Y0-EIX-914

P

Pisgah Press

Pisgah Press was established in 2011 to publish and promote works of quality offering original ideas and insight into the human condition, the realm of knowledge, and the world around us.

Copyright © 2014 Jeff Messer

Printed in the United States of America

Published by Pisgah Press, LLC
PO Box 1427, Candler, NC 28715
www.pisgahpress.com

Book & cover design: A. D. Reed, MyOwnEditor.com

All rights reserved. No part of this publication may be reproduced, stored in a retrieval system, or transmitted, in any form or by any means, electronic, mechanical, photocopying, recording, or otherwise, without the prior written permission of Pisgah Press, except in the case of quotations in critical articles or reviews.

Library of Congress Cataloging-in-Publication Data
Messer, Jeffrey Douglas
Red-state, White-guy Blues/Messer

Library of Congress Control Number: 2014955490

ISBN-13: 978-1942016045
Political Science/Government/Commentary

First Edition
First Printing
November 2014

Acknowledgements

There are far too many people to thank, without forgetting some names, but I will certainly try.

I'm lucky to be on air three hours a day, and communicate with so many people, as we all seek the truth in this age of confusion. My listeners and callers are among the smartest people I've ever encountered. And, while I've met many of them, there are many, many more whom I know only by their voice.

Thanks so much for embracing me, and making what I do feel all the more special: Mike, Greyhawk, David, the other David, Matt, Sue, Terri, Frank, Ron, Sue, Susan, Sarah, Harry, Brother Darrow, Gregory, Boyd, Linda, Catherine, Hawkeye, Terry, Sam, the other Sam, Randy, Claire from NJ, Carol from Ohio, Michael, Tom, Dr. Franklin, Jan, Rick, Mojo Bear, and even the obnoxious right-wing caller-trolls like... well, you know who you are! And, how could I not mention the wild man, Peter Choyce, who drove from Hollywood, CA to Asheville in 2013, and the first Progressive Radio show he heard the whole trip was mine.

I am also lucky to have a great team around me at iHeart Asheville, and thank them for letting me in the door everyday, and all the good humor and camaraderie that I get from each and every one of them. But I do need to make special mention of those whom I work with the most closely: Program Director Brian Hall, Web-mistress Jessica Lee, right-leaning Pete Kaliner, Sam Steele, and my two producers extraordinaire, Seth Stewart and Jim Meyer. Also, special thanks to Local Edge Radio revolutionary trailblazers Blake Butler and Leslie Groetsch, and my sometimes back-ups, Vonciel Baudouin and Dr. Errington Thompson.

And, of course, my wonderful, sexy wife, Kelli, and Nicholas, Latham, and Mary Grace, who make it easy to find the inspiration to want to be the best I can be, and then reach even higher.

JEFF MESSER'S

RED-state, WHITE-guy BLUES

Jeff Messer

<u>Messer</u> (German for "knife," also *großes Messer* "great knife," *Hiebmesser* "hewing knife," *Kriegsmesser* "war knife," etc.) during the German Late Middle Ages and Renaissance (14th to 16th centuries) was a term for the class of single-edged bladed weapons, deriving from the medieval falchion and preceding the modern sabre.

—Wikipedia

<u>Messerism</u>: Sharp, cutting, or witty saying.

—I made this up

CHAPTERS

1. The Backstory 1
2. Asheville: Land of Peace, Arts, and Beer 9
3. Nov. 4, 2008: The Day Racism Should Have Died 11

Real Life update #1 17

4. Tea Party Rising 19
5. Don't Fear the Reaper: Fear the Census-keeper 21
6. Land of the Straight (and Narrow) 23
7. Puppet Pat, Stringing the Voters Along 25

Real Life Update #2: Radio Free Me 27

8. Payback Time 31

Local News Briefs 37

Real Life Update #3: 39

Tight-fitting National Briefs #1: Test-driving the Police State 43

9. Moral Mondays: Protest Done Right 45
10. Water Wars: Raleigh v. Asheville 51
11. A Few Local Heroes? Check! 59
12. ...and the Legion of Doom 71
13. Moral Mondays Hit the Road 81
14. How to Poison a Neighborhood in 10 Easy Steps 87

Tight-fitting National Briefs #2 91

15. Zen and the Art of Vagina Maintenance 93

Tight-fitting National Briefs #3 95

16. West Carolina, an Old New Idea 97

Tight-fitting National Briefs #4 103

Real-Life Update #4: 105
17 ObamaCare Scorn, and I Don't Care 111
18 Everything Else from 2013 in 10 Easy Bullet Points 119
19 Money Talks. Lack of Money Screams 123
20 The (Mis-)education of Puppet Pat 131
21 Voter Wrongs, from the Right 141
Tight-fitting National Briefs #5: Stats 151
Real-Life Update #5: Kelli and I Get Married 153
22 Give a Pollute, Not a Hoot! 155
23 Raleigh & Gomorrah: Real Morality Comes to the Capital ... 157
24 Drone, Baby, Drone 161
25 Giddyup, Little Brony 165
Tight-fiting National Briefs #6: High Times 169
26 Frack You, You Fracked-up Frackers 171
27 Primary Focus Was Secondary 181
Real-Life Updates #6 183
28 The Summer So Far: NC 2014 187
29 Mountain Moral Mondays II 189
Tight-fitting National Briefs #7: 'Round & 'Round We Go 197
30 The Long Road Ahead 213
31 Electile Dysfunction 219
Epilogue 225
About the Author

Messerism #1

I'm a firm believer that the two-party system of mutual enablers needs to be destroyed. However, there's a very specific order in which we have to get it done. First, split the GOP in two (and God bless the Tea Party: they're doing a dandy job of it, if only the Democrats will stand back, shut up, and get out of their way). Then go after the Dems.

You can't do it the other way around. If the GOP wins even one election cycle with total dominance (e.g., Florida, North Carolina, Wisconsin), they go full-on fascist. It's in their DNA. They just can't help themselves from imposing an oligarchy and calling it capitalism.

ONE
THE BACKSTORY

Who am I?
How did I get here ...
and how did I end up this way?

Words to ponder ... if that sort of navel-gazing is up your alley. And living in Asheville, I could get away with it, should I choose.
But I'm actually talking about it in literal terms.

Who am I?

Jeff Messer. Native of Waynesville, North Carolina, 30 miles west and about 10 years back from Asheville. Radio-talk-show host, with my own Progressive talk show from 3 to 6 p.m. weekdays on *880 The Revolution*, broadcast on 880 AM and iHeart Radio. I've been doing the radio show only since the beginning of 2013, but I've got a long career in the entertainment business behind me.

How did I get here?

As I said, I was born pretty close to Asheville, on October 27, 1970, and spent my childhood just half an hour away. But the path from there to here wasn't quite direct. I traveled a bit in the early '90s, after my year off from high school to "find myself" ended six months in, with my getting involved in a local community theater (now The Haywood Arts Regional Theatre, or HART) and winding up with an offer to tour as an actor. I spent a few years on the road, doing shows off and on in a number of states, and eventually heading to Edinburgh, Scotland for the Edinburgh Festival Fringe in August of 1993.

Jeff Messer

I attended college from 1994 to 1998 at Western Carolina University, studying theatre. Along the way, I pursued my path as a writer, seeing several of my plays produced and one achieving "Regional Second Runner-Up" for the Kennedy Center College Short Play Competition. That's a bit like getting a bronze medal in the Olympics: bragging rights galore, but very few Nike endorsement deals coming your way.

In 2000, I finally moved to Asheville, as the city started to become a major creative-arts type of place. And, in the decade that followed, happily, it became all that, and even more than I had hoped for.

I had been somewhat politically oriented during the 1990s and became more so during the 2000s. How could one not, having witnessed the ascension of the witless George W. Bush—and all the controversy that came with him—and the chaos he soon wrought?

I started doing my own little blog in 2004, which was mostly a political ranting place. Then, in 2006, I was the second-place winner (again, no Nike deals) of a regional Radio Talk-Show Host competition sponsored by the now-defunct Air America.

Six years later, I would have my very own talk show (right place, right time, and all that.)

My stage play, *This War Is Live*, a tale of a documentary filmmaker during the first year of the Iraq War, debuted in Charleston, SC in 2008 at the Footlight Theatre, and was mounted again for the Piccolo Spoleto Festival that year.

Once I made my way to radio, I found myself neck-deep in an oddly turning tide of political insanity in my beloved home state, when NC, for the first time in nearly 150 years, fell under total GOP control ... and the worst-case scenarios all started to come to pass.

Which leads me to this book.

How did I end up this way?

Living in NC—hell, living in the Deep South—and having been born in the era after the desegregation of the 1960s, I should have ended up as another Good Ol' Southern Republican Redneck. Truly. I was born among, and spent most of my life, surrounded by them.

But I was an odd child. Perhaps born in the wrong place (though definitely not the wrong time, as I feel lucky to live in this era.)

The tale that my mother often told was one of me being a two-year-old little chatterbox, but also being creative from an early age. So much so that she had taken to putting a book in my hands as I sat perched in the shopping cart while she was out buying the week's groceries.

But I couldn't read. Obviously. I mean, I was only two: an illiterate toddler. So instead of reading, I would start to tell the story of the book aloud as I followed the pictures.

Now, you might think that it would be mostly gibberish, coming from such a small child. But according to my mother, my interpretations were so impressive that on one occasion an elderly man stopped his wife and marveled to her: "Look! That baby is reading that book!"

Needless to say, I may have been destined to be a storyteller from that point forward.

I grew up in rural farming country, with lots of good ol' boys (and girls) in my family and in my immediate sphere of influence. But my main source of inspiration seemed to come from being plopped down in front of an old black-and-white TV in my grandmother's living room to watch all those great game shows that used to air in the mornings: *The Price Is Right*, *Pyramid*, *Jokers Wild*, etc. Apparently, I learned more of my diction from those shows than from those around me. Not sure what that does to the "nurture versus nature" theory.

Whatever it was, it led to my actually correcting the adults around me when they would use bad grammar, or misspeak. Most notably, at age five, correcting an adult's pronunciation of the word "briar," which they pronounced "brar" (rhymes with "star"). Cute, yes. Popular? Not so much, maybe.

At the age of nine I was enamored with Ronald Reagan. The Hollywood charmer-turned-president was the first president I really took note of. The Iran hostage situation was in the news, and Ronnie was the superhero who saved the day. All I recall noticing was that after he won, the hostages were freed. So he seemed like a super-duper, awesome, groovy president, at least to me—and millions of other gullible Americans, though they weren't nine years old.

Fortunately, by the time Iran-Contra hit, I had grown out of my brief,

3

youthful crush on the GOP.

Not entirely unrelated, I was a good little Southern Baptist kid, too. Some great years, with some really nice people. A lot of fun growing up in a little country church. Until I was sixteen and started to notice how many people were paying so much attention to each other, and gossiping, and doodling, that they weren't listening to the sermon. It seemed a little disconcerting to me that all these nice "Christians" were busy with all the details of everything other than the real message. Then—maybe not right away, but soon enough—I realized that I was doing the same thing, by paying more attention to them than the minister. So, I started to pay attention. And when I heard the message being delivered, I realized that the tactics of organized religion were not something I agreed with.

I never went back after that, deciding that true spirituality, and true morality and understanding, would be greater if I could find it without the scare tactics and guilt trips of the church.

It is amazing how freeing that was. No longer being a willing "sheep" in the flock of the Southern Baptist Church (where we're all told that we are supposed to be good little sheep, by the way) liberated me from other such sheep-like tendencies, which, oddly enough, seemed to be the formula for political party affiliation.

In 1992, I was more of a fan of Jerry Brown than Bill Clinton, but I knew for sure I was not a fan of George H. W. Bush, who had given us—among other things—Clarence Thomas and the Gulf War.

The latter of which sent a bunch of local National Guardsmen off to the front lines on day one. Mind you, these were mostly middle-aged men with families who had already served in the last war, in Vietnam. Among them was a close friend and high-school teacher of mine named Preston, who chose to stand up as a conscientious objector against the military action itself, and even more so against sending these middle-aged family men in first. (Testing the strength of the enemy, perhaps, with some cannon fodder?)

Seeing the reality close up was enough to extinguish any lingering Republicanism that may have been smoldering under the surface.

But I was kind of a fan of Ross Perot, as well. How could you not love that mad bastard? And, if you think about it, he is still a shining example of the kind of third-party spoiler we need in politics. He was a serious contender, and therefore a threat to both the Democrats and the Republicans. Rambling Ross just got a little too crazy for most of us. Which is a bit ironic, given how the Tea Party today has filled that spoiler void, but they've been conscripted by the GOP (which won't let the Perot factor happen again) to humorous, and potentially even disastrous, effect.

Fast-forward through the Clinton years and the coming of the modern era of partisan gridlock: we saw how petty and lunatic the GOP could become when, $41-million dollars and one Ken Starr investigation later, the prudish nature of a perpetually backward-looking party gave us a stained blue dress, a lot of tongue-wagging, and a collective shrug from the majority of America. Mind you, the booming tech sector and the rise of get-rich-quick day-traders on the stock market certainly helped salve the scandal of extra-marital dalliances by a man who had been nicknamed "Slick Willy" long before being elected to higher office. Twice.

The only good thing that came out of the whole Lewinsky scandal, as far as I'm concerned, is the one joke I wrote—back when I had some thoughts of being a stand-up comedian in the style of Dennis Miller (don't get me started on Dennis). Here's that joke:

"The Ken Starr investigation is starting to get pretty desperate to find anything they can to take down President Clinton. I just read that they've started to subpoena people who applied for the White House intern program but didn't make it in—because they apparently blew their interview."

Not genius, by any stretch, but not bad, right? For a former Southern Baptist Republican, anyway.

Once Clinton was on his way out, along came the straw that may have broken America's back: the election of 2000. The election that was ultimately decided by the United States Supreme Court set off a trend of partisanship on the Court that we are still feeling today.

I have long believed that Al Gore would have lost handily to John McCain in 2000. I think there were few people out there who didn't think that. Then the miracle happened: the GOP, in all their infinite, backward-thinking wisdom, picked George W. Bush—son of the hapless George H.W.—to be their standard-bearer.

Somehow, this born-again, dried-up drunkard, multiply-failed businessman, coked-up ne'er-do-well goofball was just what the party needed. It was the aw-shucks approach that suckered them. That and the fact that he was a severe sinner who had found salvation—even if it was well into adulthood. Some voters just can't resist that. He appeared humble, if a bit dopey, and was the furthest thing from the smooth, Slick-Willy personality that had confounded the GOP for eight long years.

Now, Al Gore should have won easily against Dubya, but he was his own worst enemy. It ended up a too-close-to-call election night. And over a month later, it came down to the one-seat partisan divide on the Supreme Court, establishing them as just another branch of the government that had been corrupted by politics.

What followed was eight years of chaos, corruption, war crimes, erosion of civil liberties, and the sunset of America's greatness.

Had McCain been the GOP nominee and won the 2000 election, we would be living in quite a different world today.

Back then, McCain was still "The Maverick," not the grumpy old crackpot he's turned into. He was a leader in campaign finance reform efforts, and his hawkishness was more measured. Unlike Dubya, he was his own man, attuned to how politics worked from a compromise and work-together standpoint. And McCain the War Hero would not have saddled us with Cheney the Chicken Hawk for eight years.

My belief is that, had McCain won, he would have been more open to listening to people like Richard Clarke, who was trying to get the Cheney-Bush team's attention over coming threats of terrorist attack. Perhaps, under McCain, 9/11 would not have happened. And, had it not, there would have been no Iraq War to drain the nation's economy and reduce our standing in the world.

Sure, that would mean that Osama Bin Laden would still be out there, but perhaps McCain would have found smarter ways to combat the rise in terrorism. I do believe he would have been smarter about how he went about it, and would not have gotten us into unnecessary wars that were the spark that really set off the powder keg that we're contending with today.

McCain could have been a two-term Republican president of such stature that he could have ushered in a new, more moderate GOP era that might have spelled doom for the Democratic party. He could have been the greatest Republican president of the modern era, making people forget about Nixon and stop needlessly adoring Reagan. Hell, McCain could have been a majority candidate for Mount Rushmore, having pulled independents into the fold, along with most of those centrist Democrats.

A McCain presidency would also have meant that the rise of the junior Senator from Illinois, Barack Obama, would have been essentially still-born in 2004, and perhaps Obama would not even still be in the Senate today. How's that for a slap in the face to the GOP?

But no, the GOP wanted Dubya in a big, bad way. And they got him big—and the rest of us got the bad.

I've often wondered why they passed on a sure thing in McCain in favor of the gamble of Dubya. But then I look at the chaos that came with the Dubya years, and the Patriot Act, and NSA surveillance, and the economic calamity for most Americans, while corporations got a free pass and grew all the richer. Then I think about the Project for a New American Century, and all their goals, and the fact that all of those jokers had key roles in the Dubya administration, and I really don't have to wonder for very long.

They got all that they wanted, and more. And we gave it to them. And, that, roughly, is where this book begins....

Messerism #3

GOP is just God spelled with a head up its ass.

TWO
ASHEVILLE: LAND OF PEACE, ARTS, AND BEER

It is important to mention, again, that I live in Asheville, North Carolina. Yes, THAT Asheville. And, yes, it is really that cool and wonderful.

What makes Asheville so special?

That's hard to put a finger on. It's a lot of things. Most people who became aware of Asheville over the past dozen or so years know it as a town of arts and culture, and, especially now, beer. Microbrews blew up big here in the past ten years and made us the envy of the rest of the world. At least the beer-loving universe.

Be it lists like "Beer City USA," or "The Top Ten Friendliest Places in America," or "Most Beautiful Places," or various other lists, Asheville is well known for being a place that people really want to go to. And (I warn everyone out there) if you spend more than three days here, you will start making plans to relocate.

Asheville has the good fortune of being nestled in the Appalachian Mountains, but also being at the perfect point in the western part of the state. From here, you can be in South Carolina, Tennessee, Virginia, or Georgia in roughly an hour (give or take a few minutes). We're close to everything, but still isolated enough.

The people here come in all shapes, backgrounds, and beliefs. And they all seem to get along in a nice harmony. There's something special and peaceful here that makes Asheville unlike any other place I've ever found in all my travels. And it's only half an hour east (and still ten years ahead) of where I was born and raised.

If you follow election maps that break down the county-by-county results, you will notice this funky little blue dot in the mostly red areas of western North Carolina. That blue spot is Buncombe County. And that blue spot is thanks to Asheville being a peaceful, friendly, and decidedly progressive little city.

We're a tiny blue island in a vast sea teeming with red sharks.

Messerism #8

There is a big difference between the two national political parties: the GOP will always demand more of what they want, and never back down, while the Democrats show up well prepared to give in and surrender their position. And after the GOP says "no" to every compromise, and the Dems give up everything from peripherals to core principles to placate them, it's called "getting things done." Then the GOP will still bash the Dems for it.

THREE
2008: THE DAY RACISM SHOULD HAVE DIED, BUT ENDED UP COMING BACK AS A ZOMBIE

Election Day, 2008. The returns came in much earlier than anyone who had been listening to the mainstream media could have expected. They'd insisted all along that there was a real horse-race and it was going to be a down-to-the-wire affair. Hey, if the media admitted the race was over, everybody would turn off the TV—and where would their ad dollars go then?

So, it was down to the wire. Only it wasn't.

Flash back to September of 2008. I'm having lunch with my creative writing partner, Robert Akers. We're talking about script projects, and what to do with our successful stage play about Robin Hood, and plans for it. Things drift to various topics as we play catch-up with each other. And of course, conversation turns to politics.

What comes to mind is a late night sixteen years earlier, in 1992, sitting in the driveway together, after we had been out partying with our pals, and picking apart the '92 candidates. We talked Perot, and we agreed how much we liked Jerry Brown more than Bill Clinton.

This time, Robert asked me if I was nervous about the "news" reports about how much money McCain's campaign had versus Obama. I said I wasn't and explained that the big-media story is skewed so as to keep it competitive, because ratings depended on that, and revenues depend on ratings. If it were a one-sided race, people would tune out.

I also pointed to a recent, and somewhat obscure, report I'd read that showed the actual numbers of people who had given donations to McCain and Obama.

McCain, while (slightly) ahead in cash, had far fewer contributions that were under, or even close to, the maximum amount that the law allowed people to donate. In other words, he had more money, but it was big donations from a smaller number of people.

Conversely, Obama had a HUGE number of people who were donating less than $250 each to his campaign—lots and lots of people giving $20, $50, $100 to Obama. For McCain, those small donors were few and far between.

My logic was that, if someone donates, even something as small as $20, they are certainly going to vote for that candidate. And that meant that the sheer numbers of voters supporting Obama were quite a bit higher than those supporting McCain.

It may have been overly simplistic on some level, but, in the end, it proved to be true.

And, as I watched the returns come in, it was reported that North Carolina was the state that tipped the scale to Obama, followed by Colorado. (Some people will tell you that Colorado put Obama over the top, but they would be wrong.)

As that realization set in, it was quite emotional for me on a number of levels.

Now, I had not been an Obama supporter in the beginning. After an eight-year ass-whipping at the hands of George W. Bush's era of great American decay, I knew that the GOP needed to be out of the White House. At any and all cost, this nation—and the world—could not handle four, or even eight, more years of that!

I was a huge John Edwards supporter. Sure, he's from NC. But that wasn't all of it. I just loved that plucky little dude—and he clearly made the right wing nervous. He was a populist threat who spoke to long-dormant Southern Democrat instincts. These were the good ol' folks who had been duped into voting for the GOP and against their own interests for decades, and Edwards spoke their language.

Mind you, we all discovered later why John Edwards was not a good pick. For those with short memories: he ended up getting caught for screwing some lady who was not his wife (who was dying of cancer at the time) and fathering a child, then trying to cover it up.

I think that the prudes out there are wrong more than they are right. And clearly they will forgive someone they like for such sins, if he shows enough of that "aw-shucks" sincerity in his apology.

At least if they're Republicans, anyway. Who can forget—no matter how hard we try—Mark Sanford, the former South Carolina governor who lied about "hiking the Appalachian Trail" while flying off to Argentina to be with his mistress. He came back and was reelected to his old Congressional seat! Why? It was "true love," which apparently trumps misuse of taxpayer funds and adultery, even in the Palmetto State. I just wish that they would at least nickname some peak on the Appalachian Trail "Sanford's Knob."

And what about Davd Vitter, Louisiana toe-sucker. Or Strom Thurmond, fathering a child with the black maid. Or....

John Edwards—aside from giving the strongest "thumbs up" gesture of any modern politician—was a smooth-talking, syrupy sweet Southern-drawled do-gooder, and he was a serious contender in 2004 and 2008.

Next up was NY Senator and former First Lady Hillary Clinton. In spite of the baggage, she was, and still is, a real competitor. More than enough American similarities to the UK's Iron Lady, Maggie Thatcher, but slightly more progressive and a little less of a ball-buster. And Hillary, of course, comes with Bill, who would be the first First Gentleman of the United States. Talk about something that would make some aged, angered, wrinkly old GOP heads explode. Picture Bill in bathrobe, coming out in the morning onto the White House steps to fetch the morning paper, waving to the people. Imagine him slipping into the White House tours on a regular basis, bringing the pretty girls out back with him for a Bubba Barbeque and kegger.

Yeah, just thinking about those images would pretty much kill half of the senior GOP elected officials. Not First Gentleman; First Bubba. And Bill would do it. You know he would.

So once John Edwards was out, I threw my support to Hillary. Nothing against Obama. I liked the way he talked, maybe even more than Clinton. But I knew that the Democrats HAD TO WIN the 2008 election. And, after eight years of Dubya, were the Dems stupid enough to risk it all by going for the farthest gamble between to two pretty big ones: the potential first woman president, or the first non-white male president? Either way, if the Dems won, history was going to be made. I just wasn't convinced that America was ready to take the big racial

13

step, especially considering how far to the right things had swung in the preceding few years.

I was worried.

And, then, McCain was the GOP standard-bearer. John "The Maverick" McCain! The dude who would have won in 2000 against Gore, without a recount!

Holy shit. It was over.

Then McCain picked Sarah Palin as a running mate. And, yes, it was over.

Back to election night 2008:

My first thoughts went to my five-year-old son, Nicholas. Poor kid had been subjected to progressive radio in the car most of his life. And, yes, I did teach him to say "Barack rocks, McCain's insane" just to irritate his conservative Grandpa.

To me, in that moment, it didn't matter if Obama was a success. All he had to do was stop the hemorrhaging that Dubya had started. Sure, it would be great if he could come in and magically heal the nation, and resurrect America from the smoldering heap that it had been driven to by power-hungry, war-mongering, greedy, morally corrupt leaders.

But in that moment, I realized the true importance of Obama that would live on whether he succeeded in office or not. He was the first non-white man to hold the office. Okay, he was half-white, but that didn't matter, as the only thing the haters would see what his African American heritage.

The true importance of Obama was something that would be gained from the perspective of my five-year-old son. Obama would be the first president that Nicholas—or any other child born after 9/11—would remember. Their first president would be a non-white, mixed-race, literally African-and-American guy from Hawaii—the last state admitted to the Union. Appropriate, isn't it?

When Nicholas is able to vote in the election of 2022, he will have grown up in a world where race, so far as who can become president, does not exist. And, should he encounter some grumpy, 90-year-old, backward-thinking Republican who says that a minority or a woman can't be president, my son will look at this faded and fading person like he's out of his mind.

And he would be right.

Of course, it would not take long after the 2008 election before those old, backward people would rear their heads in a death rattle of hate and ignorance, in an attempt to keep the poisons of the 20th century alive and well in a 21st century they won't long inhabit.

Suddenly, there were people who were upset about the decline of the economy and of America's standing in the world. Mind you, I, along with millions of progressives, had been screaming about the decline since around 2002, but these people—THESE people—didn't seem to notice or care until after Obama won and stepped up to fix the mess. And then, man, oh man, did they care! Outrage! Teabags! Oh, my!

I was happy to finally see them get on the same page where so many of us had been for half a decade already, but I had a sneaking feeling that they weren't quite swift enough to give credit where it was due.

Nope. They were hell-bent on picket-sign-lynching the black guy who'd just got elected.

And, so, the death of racism that we saw trumpeted into place in early November of 2008, and celebrated with passion and joy in late January of 2009, gave way within weeks to the gnawing, clawing, moaning rise of racist Zombies, who would make an episode of *The Walking Dead* look like *I Love Lucy*.

Messerism #69

The Tea Party claims to not harbor any racism in its ranks. They also like to claim to not be overtly partisan, despite having been bought and paid for by one particular political party. Of course, they say that it didn't start out that way. And certainly, since they started in early 2009, they were indeed protesting W-era policies, since no Obama policies had taken effect. Though I'm having a hard time finding any of those original Tea Party protest signs that showed images of Dubya as The Joker from The Dark Knight *in a lab coat, or those oh-so-famous Dubya-as-a-Witch-Doctor-with-a-bone-through-his-nose signs.*

REAL LIFE UPDATE #1

While 2008 would be a year of renewed hope for many progressives, it would be a time of great difficulty for me on a personal level, as my marriage fell apart and I found myself having to rebuild my own life from the ground up, at the same time that America as a whole was looking forward to turning the page.

Despite the great hope and inspiration to be found in the rise of Obama, in my own life, hope and joy were the furthest thing from reality.

Nicholas was born in 2003. His mother and I were married in 2005. We split in 2008, after a nine-year relationship.

In many ways, my relationship with Nicholas's mother had been filled with ups and downs. It was never easy. We struggled. We had a baby—unplanned. We ran a small independent theater in the early days of the growth of Asheville. Against all odds, and defying logic, we managed to make a go of it.

Oddly enough, in 2008, things were looking up for us, and improving. For the first time, it looked as if the struggles were behind us.

Then it was no more. At 37, I had to start over. And it was a giant pain in the ass.

As if powers beyond my control were determined that I was going to come out of this stronger, great opportunities greeted me—though, admittedly, I was stubbornly reluctant to be happy, or anything resembling it.

In 2009, I wrote a play for Parkway Playhouse (a professional theater I had been associated with for a few years) about an African American musician from the 1920s and '30s named Lesley Riddle.

Riddle had been friends with A.P. Carter of the Carter Family, the "First Family of Country Music" since the early days of radio. Riddle had helped find the Carters and recorded some of their biggest hits. It was Riddle's connection to the Appalachian songs passed down through oral tradition that gave the Carters the material to fill their early performances and music catalogue.

Riddle, nicknamed Esley, was missing his right leg below the knee and two middle fingers on his strumming hand. That "finger deficiency" was one of the things that made his sound unique: a sound that was made famous by Maybelle Carter, who got the acclaim and credit. In the 1960s, in an interview with Maybelle, Mike Seeger asked her about her playing style, and she told him about Riddle.

After a search, Seeger found Riddle and recorded a series of interviews and performances, which were the first and only actual recordings of Riddle playing the songs as he originally knew them.

It was a marvelous tale. And, in light of the Obama election victory, it was more timely than ever.

The show world-premiered on July 30, 2009, to critical acclaim and sold-out audiences.

Out of a dark place came a wonderful success, and a new door of opportunity opened.

During the press tour to promote the show, I appeared on the radio program *Local Edge Radio*, broadcast on 880 The Revolution in Asheville. It was the very studio and the very show that I would inherit in early 2013, when I became the local Progressive Radio Talk Show host.

Funny how things work themselves out, whether you want them to or not, or are even trying to make it happen.

Messerism #14

I just love seeing that bleary-eyed-reaction moment when you tell a Tea Party member that it's hot tea, and not iced. Want to make them cry? Also mention that it's not sweet but very bitter to drink.

FOUR
TEABAGGING: It's Not Just for Kinky Couples and Porn Stars Anymore

Somebody out there saw something in those Tetley teabag-wearing mad hatters. They saw a frenzy of low-information, high-anxiety, willful ignorance that needed to be brought into some degree of balance with the force that is the GOP machine.

Faster than you can say "Koch Brothers check book," the Tea Party joined the Grand Old Party, assured that their hate and mis-assigned scapegoatery of Obama would not go untapped—or unrewarded.

Of course, no one told the Tea Party that they were an inconvenient lack of truth to the GOP. And no one told them that the money that was thrown their way to join the team was also meant to put them in their own special place. A quiet place. In the corner. To be seen, but not heard. Kind of like that child born of an unfortunate roll in the hayloft between a pair of Mississippi cousins, who turn out to be brother and sister instead. Shhh. We don't talk about little Slappy, over there. God bless him. A gift from Jesus, and we didn't get a receipt, so can't take him back.

Well, it shouldn't have been all that surprising that the Tea Party folks didn't get the memo. Or they didn't read it. Or they couldn't read. (Still not sure where the communication broke down.)

And, once they were allowed under the big circus tent filled with elephants and clowns, those silly Tea-totalers thought their opinions were just as important as those of their corporate/capitalist Republican masters. Which led them to start speaking up. Loudly, proudly, and with all the intellectual credibility of Sarah Palin after taking too many meds.

The horrible lack of foresight resulted in actual Tea Party Republicans getting elected all over the place in 2010—a moment that sent ripples through the establishment wing of the establishment party. And it caught many a Democrat by complete, slack-jawed surprise.

Including the proud state that had helped usher in the era of Obama by going surprisingly blue in 2008: North Carolina.

Messerism #37

The last time there we saw an unlikely relationship as perfect as the GOP and the Tea Party was Michael Douglas and Glenn Close in Fatal Attraction. *And we all know how that turned out.*

FIVE
Don't Fear the Reaper, Fear the Census keeper!

2010: Time for the Census once again! Lots of part-time jobs for the long-term unemployed were being posted all around. You see, as is our tradition, every so often we do a little head-count in the nation, and, when needed, we redraw district lines to reflect the new numbers. This keeps track of our population growth, as well as strives to keep elections and representation somewhat fair.

By this point, the Tea Party had been around for about a year. And, thanks to some Koch cash, they had quickly stopped being a new and independent political movement, and were now a wholly owned subsidiary of the GOP. (Psst ... Don't tell them; they're in denial.) And with all that cash and motiv-hate-tion, Tea Party Republicans would win a surprising number of elections in 2010. This new Pepto-inducing movement had ramifications far and wide across the country.

Here in The Old North State, the Tea Party takeover was huge. It seemed to come out of nowhere and take even the most politically astute by surprise. The state found itself going from a pleasant, New-South shade of Tarheel blue to a deep, dangerous, and eerily throwback shade of red, taking us back toward an era we had thought we were long past.

How did it happen in NC, the state that made the difference in 2008? How could we slip back so far, so fast?

I point you to the Census of 2010.

If you recall, from those Tea Party corners of the Republican Party came scare talk that would make McCarthy stop and say, "Whoa now. Let's take a breath and think about this." They talked about the evils of the Census. They talked about dark, ugly ObamAmerica's attempt to implant chips in every citizen as a way to control us. They told people that the Census was a conspiracy. It was a trap that even Admiral Ackbar wouldn't have seen coming, to track us and create files about us all. Surely, it was a lead-up to concentration camps that Obama would instruct FEMA to open, where all white people, all church people, and all who dared to speak out against the darkening of America at the hands of a Manchurian Kenyan candidate who was going to bring about the end of all of America's hopes and dreams.

Yeah. That.

Course, they didn't talk about the fact that the Constitution—our (much-amended) founding document they want to "take America back" for—mandates a Census every ten years. They probably didn't know it.

Crazy talk about the Census was heard far and wide. "Chase the Obama Census takers off your land" was heard everywhere by Teabaggers. Because Fear. Works. Every. Time.

But, as a result of that same terrifying Census that followed the 2010 election, North Carolina redrew district lines. And, not surprisingly, the new lines favored the GOP. So much so that by the 2014 election year, the number of Blue votes to Red votes it takes to elect someone to Congress from NC stands at an average of 3.2 to 1.

Could it be that the crazy Tea Party, tinfoil-hat conspiracy theorists accidentally opened the door for a more far-reaching GOP takeover in NC? Or could they have been so politically savvy to have out-witted everyone, by setting the table for said GOP takeover?

In the end, it doesn't matter how they did it. They did it. And, in 2012, the full takeover from the far right would be complete.

Messerism #22

Life, liberty and the pursuit of happiness doesn't have an asterisk after it, with a list of people, races, and beliefs that are not included. Despite what the GOP seems to think.

SIX
LAND OF THE STRAIGHT (AND NARROW)

Oh, To Be Gay, Now That Spring Is Here!

Thanks to the Tea Party, and their trunk full of ignorance and fears going mainstream in 2010, the thought-to-be-dormant (think *Godzilla* sequels) concept of needing to pass constitutional amendments that prohibit same-sex marriage (even in places where it was already illegal) reared its head in North Carolina.

In the spring of 2012, a proposed constitutional amendment was put to the voters. Amendment One was scheduled for the May primary, when a huge Republican turnout was expected to choose a GOP gubernatorial candidate to challenge whomever the Democrats picked to succeed Governor Bev Perdue. It worked.

I'm happy to report that voters in Buncombe County (thanks to Asheville) rejected doubling down on the ban: here, the vote tally was roughly 70% to 30% against. However, in most of the rest of the state, and in surrounding counties, those numbers were flipped.

So Amendment One passed. Well, thanks to approximately 70% of the 34% voter turnout (23.8%). In other words just over one fifth of the state's voters. Ah, math.

Of course, by the next year, a massive number of other states around the nation started going in the exact opposite direction, eliminating previous restrictions and, finally, allowing same-sex couples to wed. Some found that path on their own, but others were emboldened by the Supreme Court's 5-4 ruling striking down the Defense of Marriage Act on June 26, 2013.

In spite of the tide clearly rolling in the opposite direction, North Carolina joined the dwindling number of states fighting to deny marriage to legal citizens.

In fact, thanks to this, in 2013, many same-sex couples in NC had gone to other states to legally marry, yet were being instructed by tax-preparers and officials that, even though they were filing federal returns as married, they had to lie on state returns and file as single.

Maybe it's just me, but I smelled a serious trap in this. The State of North Carolina told citizens to knowingly lie on their tax returns. Which, is, of course, illegal, especially if it can be proven that one has willfully falsified tax documents.

But, that's North Carolina. Logic, compassion, and common sense are endangered in this state.

Messerism #10

Both political parties need the issues more than they need the resolutions on most of the controversial topics. Take abortion, for example. Republicans don't want to overturn Roe v. Wade, *despite how much the right wing say they do. As it stands, they get just enough votes and contributions from the single-issue voters who are anti-abortion; if the issue went away, so too would those narrow voters—and their dollars. Similar practices are carried out over their other favorite issues as well: gays and guns.*

SEVEN
PUPPET PAT, STRINGING THE VOTERS ALONG

Final solidification of Tea Party influence in North Carolina came with the 2012 election. The 2010 vote had set the table, gerrymandering after the hated 2010 Census had provided an appetizer, and now it was time to serve up the main meal.

Enter Pat McCrory, seven-term mayor of Charlotte and long-time (29 years) employee of Duke Energy. A self-professed moderate, he charmed his way through the right cocktail parties and Rotary Club functions and sold—or snowed—almost everyone. He assured voters he was not a typical Republican, not a right-winger, just a pragmatic coalition-building businessman: he would be his own man. And while no one was looking, he knelt down to North Carolina's red-shoed, mitred Pope (see Chapter Eight) and pledged subservience and fealty in exchange for bags full of cash.

In a perfect world, the walkless talk of Pat McCrory would be great. Unless, of course, he was more full of shit than good intentions and integrity. Guess which way it ended up?

The Tea Party had gained control of all other levels of state government, even the courts. The only prize left was the governor's mansion, crown, and throne.

McCrory won, and the headlines touted the uncomfortable fact that his victory marked the first time in nearly 150 years that the GOP controlled all levels of government in NC. A dubious honor at best.

Before the election, minority Democrats in the General Assembly may not have viewed their positions as being akin to the last week at the Alamo, but following the takeover, I'm sure they were all looking at their coonskin caps and Bowie knives with a growing sense of impending doom.

Among the lone defenders of the left was Democratic Attorney

General Roy Cooper, who soon after the takeover began to set up the dominoes for his own run at the governorship in 2016. Never mind that he would have four long years of a daunting fight ahead of him before this would even be on the menu.

Messerism #52

If you haven't figured out that most of the GOP say one thing to get votes, then do the bidding of their wealthy benefactors, then you're not paying attention. And based on some things that come out of the mouths of the GOP politicians, either they're stupid, or they think the voters are stupid. Or both. Neither of which should be acceptable scenarios to any of us.

REAL LIFE UPDATE #2

My radio career began as something of a forgotten dream come true. I had been politically aware for many years, and during the Dubya era, I really ramped up my anger at what had gone wrong with the system and the country.

But back in the early 2000s, there was no Progressive Talk Radio. Only Right-Wing Radio.

So, I blogged some. First on Yahoo 360 (how's that for old?), then on MySpace (and how sad is it that THAT feels old now?).

I used to listen to NPR, but on the day after the 2004 election, I switched to our local AM station 880 The Revolution, which carried many Air America shows, from Marc Maron & Mark Riley doing a morning show to Al Franken in the afternoon. Eventually Rachel Maddow would grace the 880 air waves, as would Thom Hartmann, Stephanie Miller, Bill Press, Randi Rhodes, and Ed Schultz.

And in 2006, Air America held a competition for wannabe new radio show hosts. I entered through 880 and got to compete with ten other folks, including Errington Thompson and future Asheville City Council member Cecil Bothwell. (Errington had a weekend show on 880, called "Where Is The Outrage?" and a blog of the same name—still active at WhereIsTheOutrage.com—and he writes a monthly op-ed column for Asheville's *The Urban News*. He became a great guest host and friend of my show. For more on Cecil, keep reading.)

But I didn't win. Cecil did. The consolation was being told that I was second pick.

At any rate, that was about the time that 880 decided to air its own local progressive talk show from 3 to 6 p.m. It was called Local Edge Radio, and like a lot of other area progressives, I tuned in regularly.

Then, six years later, in the aftermath of the 2012 election, things were looking dark for North Carolina. And that very December, after the election but before the changing of the guard in Raleigh, I learned that Local Edge Radio's host, Blake Butler, was leaving the show to pursue other career paths. I had met Blake in 2009 and kept up with him and the show over the years. I had came on from time to time to promote theater work I was doing, and once—April 20, 2012—he invited me to co-host the show with him.

When I heard that Blake was stepping down, I emailed him, and he suggested I contact the Program Director of 880 The Revolution, Brian Hall, and have a conversation about my coming onboard and taking over the show.

Three weeks later, the newly re-branded *The Jeff Messer Show* was on the air.

My first week on the air, Pat McCrory took his oath of office as governor. And with him, a vile horde descended upon the chambers of power and quickly began to pass questionable, morally dubious laws that were, unfortunately, unstoppable, thanks to a veto-proof, opposition-proof hard-right majority. These people were so far to the right they were well past what any political junkie would even call Republican.

I remember railing against them as they took control and started announcing their plans. And that very day, I got a call from a listener who asked me how I could condemn them and their actions without seeing what they were going to do? I should perhaps give them a chance.

I answered that I based my "rage against their machine" on what they boldly said they were planning to do. I took them at their word. And their word was going to lead to a massive downfall for NC.

This—this book, right now—is the long-awaited moment when I say to that caller: "I told you so."

In fact, the GOP takeover has been far worse than anyone could have imagined. They took power and went into scorched-earth mode, leading to the quickest case of buyer's remorse since Scott Walker inspired the Wisconsin statehouse protests in the dead of winter the January after he won.

Sometimes they don't have to tell you that they plan to be raging assholes for you to know.

Sometimes they do tell you they plan to be raging assholes, and people still vote for them. Go figure.

Worth quoting

"A revolution is coming—a revolution which will be peaceful, if you are wise enough; compassionate if we care enough; successful if we are fortunate enough. But a revolution is coming whether we will it or not. We can affect its character; we cannot alter its inevitability."

—Robert F. Kennedy
Speech at the U. of Pennsylvania
May 6, 1964

It sure is coming from a ways off, since it hasn't gotten here yet from the 1960s.

Messerism #19

The Religious Right keep talking about wanting Jesus to come back. It's a good thing he didn't show up between 2002 and 2008. If he had, and had walked up to the White House—looking all Middle Eastern like he did—you know Cheney would have had him sent to Gitmo to be waterboarded.

EIGHT
Hey GOP! You Just Won NC for the First Time in Over a Century! Going to Disney World? Nope. Just Going To Wreck the State. *Payback Time!*

It didn't take long for the moderate McCrory to show his true colors: green. As in money. As in the money that Art Pope (a mini-me Koch wanna-be, inheritor of Daddy's millions) paid to get him into office.

Take empty talk of moderation, add a dash of cash, a huge stock portfolio of dirty energy interests, then blend on high for fifteen seconds, and you have instant Puppet Pat, poured into the governor's mansion. Let stand for four years until it hardens.

Art Pope became the new Guv's Budget Director, since he's the man with the money—and the plan. And that plan? To roll hard and fast to the farthest right. How far right? So far to the right that commentators and political junkies, and even regular folks, from all across the country and even around the world, sat up and noticed.

Early on, emboldened by victory, some of the folks in the GOP bragged openly that it was time for some long overdue payback. After all, the GOP had not had full control in NC since the late 1800s. Yes, the 19th century. Which is appropriate, since many of their sensibilities were popular and acceptable, even legally required, in that era (though held by Jim-Crow Democrats at the time).

Nearly 150 years had passed since the progressive, reformist, anti-KKK GOP ran NC. Sure, there had been moments where they held the Governor's seat, or the Senate, or the House. But not all three at once. And, man, oh man, by the time they won in 2012, they were drooling like Pavlov's hounds from hell responding to the dinner bell. And they were a very different party from their 19th-century ancestors.

One has to question people's policies when their primary goal is payback, rather than legislation. Until they prove that they're going to legislate their payback plans into state law. And, despite claims that they would be moderate (I'm looking at you, Pat McCrory) so as to appeal to the public desire for moderation and common sense, the game plan was quickly clear for this new alignment in NC.

The fiscally conservative pledges felt all the more hollow (more so than usual) when McCrory immediately gave his staff a huge raise. He gave his team an 8% pay bump over the outgoing Democrat administration of Bev Perdue. Cabinet Secretaries got as much as a $13,200 increase, which is considerably higher than anything paid to typical state employees in recent years.

This from the guy who ran on fiscal restraint. Of course, he ran on a lot of other things that he also instantly abandoned upon entering the governor's mansion.

The new GOP General Assembly moved quickly with their agenda as well. Take special note of the following bullet points, as they become a major part of the pushback efforts that are soon unleashed upon the newly-elected, GOP-aligned residents of Raleigh:

- Refusal of funds for Medicaid expansion in the state, allowing said funds to be passed along to other states as a result, and causing crisis-level situations for those in NC who were dependent upon such things for their very survival. The rationale was that they didn't want to increase NC's debt to the federal government, and wanted to be fiscally responsible. Though, not unexpectedly, they placed the whole of the fiscally responsible sacrifice on the poorest and sickest in our state, while supplying tax cuts for the wealthy and giving pay raises to their staffs in Raleigh.

- Refusal of federal Emergency Unemployment funds (which also went to other states), while also slashing the length of time and amount received by those collecting their earned Unemployment Insurance. The maximum amount dropped by 35%, from $535 per week to $350 per week, and the maximum number of weeks dropped to 26. This cut went into effect July 1, 2013; then, on July 1, 2014, the number of eligible weeks dropped to 14. Meanwhile, "official" unemployment numbers dropped from 8.8% at the beginning of 2013 to 6.2% by mid-2014.

- McCrory bragged about how NC GOP policies had been proven correct, as reflected by this amazing drop in unemployment. And Fox Business "news's" Stuart Varney used those numbers to hint that McCrory should make a presidential run. Of course, the numbers are skewed (federally too) and do not include just under a quarter of a million "missing workers" whose eligibility the McCrory McCronies eliminated; counting them, the state's unemployment rate was 11.4% as of mid-2014. The GOP loves these baked numbers: they cut tens of thousands of people off the unemployment books, and push out many who were already struggling, and then then take credit for there being fewer people on the rolls, as if it were a good thing. Kind of like Dubya refusing to pay for his wars as part of the budget, and then saying, "See, they don't cost us a thing."

- In 2013 the U.S. Supreme Court loosened some of the rules about protections in voting laws that prevent racists from changing rules to disproportionately disenfranchise minorities. The Court eliminated Section 5 of the Voting Rights Act as no longer needed, because it "unfairly" picked on southern-states-with-a-history-of-racism—which, of course, no longer exist. And, as if on cue, NC, along with nearly all the other southern-states-with-a-history-of-racism, rushed to the front of the line to pass racially disenfranchising new voting laws. So much so that the entire world got collective whiplash from the rate of acceleration to take advantage of the change in rules. We have no shame here. Not any more. And no reputation left, either: headlines around the nation, and the world, announced the harsh, hard-right turn in the state, calling the new laws a rollback toward the old Jim Crow laws in the South.

- NC refused to set up a state exchange for the Affordable Care Act, making it much harder for citizens to participate and get health insurance coverage. In the Department of Huge Irony, the state was ranked fifth in the nation in enrollments for ObamaCare using the federal exchange, in spite of the GOP's ham-handed attempts to prevent or discourage people from enrolling.

- And, of course, no right-wing takeover would be complete without the fight to defund parts of public education. NC fell to 46th in the nation in teacher's pay, and things got so bad that school districts in Texas (!?!?!) of all places, began to place ads in major newspapers around the state to recruit teachers to relocate to the Lone Star State, where pay and benefits are better for brand-new teachers than they are for NC teachers who have a decade of experience.

No surprise that a lot of us Tar Heels got a little upset by some, if not all, of these new GOP "improvements" to a state that was doing pretty great already, and had a fairly solid nation reputation for being sane, well-managed, and moderate. Older people might remember that reputation, dating back to the 1960s, '70s, and '80s when North Carolina was the paragon of "The New South."

But it took only weeks, not months, for the new regime in Raleigh to erase the reputation of NC and replace it as the state that lost its mind. "What went wrong in NC" was a typical headline and sentiment by mid-2013. We were in the news, again! And not in a good way.

As a result, on April 29, 2013, a small group of concerned citizens calling themselves the "Moral Monday Movement" went to the People's House in Raleigh to lodge a complaint or two. What followed was peaceful uprising that no one saw coming, and few could have predicted the game changer it became.

Red-state, White-guy Blues

Messerism #51

If you take away access to healthcare, and you take away safety nets like Unemployment Insurance, and you take away quality public education by hurting teachers and schools by lack of support and funding, and you roll back voting rights through new laws and restrictions that make it harder for the young, the poor, the old, and minorities to vote, you might not have to win elections outright, since weakening the majority of the voting public makes it harder for them to find the time and effort to stop focusing on just surviving long enough to focus on politics. And with enough gerrymandering, you don't have to worry about the public rising up and voting you out, should they overcome the obstacles placed in their path. Of course, it's their fault for not being one of the elite and wealthy, who can buy better education, and are given preferential status from cradle to silver spoon, to trust fund, to inheritance, to deluxe mausoleum burial.

LOCAL NEWS BRIEFS

Obama Comes to Asheville. Again, and Again, and Again

There's no denying it. President Obama loves Asheville! He's been here a lot. And he loves some 12 Bones BBQ and ribs. (No doubt, the stereotype must drive the old white bastards in DC mad).

He came here before the 2008 election, and he put Asheville on the top of his schedule after his second inauguration, in 2013. On that visit, he dropped hints that he and Michelle loved Asheville, and were considering moving here after the end of his presidency.

Tongues started wagging pretty hard at that little tidbit. As a result, I was invited to call in and talk with Mark Riley on his morning radio show in New York City about the Obama visit, and about Asheville.

In the summer of 2014, citing the old stories from that visit, the rumor began making the rounds again, of the Obamas making a home purchase in Asheville.

It has yet to be fully confirmed—in fact it's regularly denied—as of this writing.

State of the state[ment]

Medicaid (or lack thereof) = Death Panels

A key part of the new GOP regime in NC involved a lot of saying "No" to a lot of things that a lot of people relied upon.

In the name of being fiscally responsible, the governor and the new legislature refused to expand Medicaid for the state's most in need.

Well, here are the fiscal results of Puppet Pat and the Tangled Strings of Service.

Savings by 2019, if NC had expanded Medicaid: $3,000,000,000
Percent of uncompensated-care costs that fall on taxpayers: 75
Annual amount lost by hospitals without expansion: $600,000,000

Jeff Messer

Remember when Sarah Palin started screeching about "Death Panels?" Turns out she was right. Only, it's not a federal thing after all, it's GOP state governments, like Puppet Pat's. Go figure.

REAL LIFE UPDATE #3

Since 2012, I had been working on a special project for the independent film production company, Legacy Films, when Theresa Phillips came to me and asked me to write the screenplay for a project very near and dear to her. She had been planning this project for well over a decade and approached me about taking her treatment and transforming it into what she would then direct, as the company's next movie.

I was flattered. She had seen several plays I had written when they were produced regionally, and she felt that I had what she had been looking for.

My history with Theresa goes back over two decades to my first film job. In 1991, she worked in casting for the movie *Last of the Mohicans*, which was shot throughout WNC. They were recruiting young, strapping men to play soldiers; at twenty years old, I was eager to sign up.

Initially, I had a pretty sweet "featured extras" role. I was among about two dozen guys who got called in to be fitted for costumes on a Saturday. We were given instructions to show up for a week-long boot camp on the following Monday, where we would learn to march, load and fire the muskets, etc.

By the time I got home, however, I got a call from the production, saying that plans were on hold, and they would get back to me.

Time passed, and I eventually spent two weeks working on location as a standard extra. Word was that some of the Native American cast members were threatening a strike, for higher pay and other various reasons. I never heard the whole tale.

Eventually, the film came out, and I was beside myself once I saw the scene where the two dozen Redcoats escort the leading ladies through the forest, whereupon they are attacked and massacred by the bad guys. The women are saved by Daniel Day Lewis and his buddies, and the movie rolled along.

I realized that I was originally going to be one of THOSE GUYS! It was deflating. So close!

Over the next few years, I kept showing up for casting calls, and kept seeing Theresa. I worked on an early Ben Stiller film for Disney called *Heavyweights*. (Stiller was a major ass to everyone, due to his directing debut, *Reality Bites*, having been the #1 movie for several weeks leading up to the shoot. Bitter, arrogant little man. I hope he's gotten better.) I also worked with Dan Ackroyd (a generous, fun, and funny man) and the late James Garner (one of the nicest "famous" people I've ever been in the same room with) in the movie *My Fellow Americans*.

After that, I drifted away from doing movie work.

In 2010 or thereabouts I ran across Theresa again, while I was working at Parkway Playhouse in Burnsville, thirty miles north of Asheville (and, like Waynesville, a few decades behind). In 2011, Parkway produced a stage version of two of my plays, *Robin Hood* (co-written with Robert Akers) and an adaptation of *Dracula* (co-written with Andrew Gall). It was just after that when Theresa approached me with her plans.

Legacy Films focuses on legends of the region, and this one was a doozy!

Did you know that there's a better-than-good chance that Abraham Lincoln was born not in Kentucky, but North Carolina? Did you know that Abraham Lincoln might not actually be a Lincoln, but rather an Enloe?

Neither did I, and I've lived here for most of my life!

It was a staggeringly intriguing story, rife with potential controversy and more than a few very passionate reactions from people who believe it, or deny it.

I was hooked. I said yes, and began researching the tales.

The basics of it are this:

Abe's mother, Nancy Hanks, was an illegitimate child, who in her early teens finds work with a prominent Rutherford County family named Enloe. As she grows into a young woman, an affair begins with the patriarch of the family. His name? Abraham Enloe.

The Enloes eventually move west toward the Cherokee lands, and it is discovered that Nancy is pregnant with Abraham's child. Scandal ensues.

Eventually, Enloe arranges for her and the newborn baby to move to Kentucky, to an arranged marriage with one Tom Lincoln.

I'll stop there, as I want to make sure you all buy tickets to see it, once it comes out.

The filming is slated to begin in late 2014 or early 2015.

It's a great story from western NC, one that few people outside of here even know about.

Messerism #113

The far right are so terrified of Obama being too black. If anything, he's gone out of his way to disprove those fears. Personally, I wish, just once, before he's out of office, he would go on vacation in December, and let his 'fro grow out just a little, get a concealed-carry permit, and buy some bling. Then show up for the State of the Union address, stroll in to some Wu Tang Clan music, take the podium and whip off his jacket, revealing a shoulder holster. Then whip the pistol out of the holster and lay it up on the podium, fist bump Biden, flash a gang sign or two at the Supreme Court, and open the speech with the Ezekiel scripture Samuel L. Jackson used in Pulp Fiction.

Talk about getting cooperation the next day from Congress. Of course, a full half of them will stroke out within the first five minutes of the SOTU speech.

TIGHT-FITTING NATIONAL BRIEFS #1
TEST-DRIVING THE POLICE STATE

April 15, 2013 was a tragic day, and not just for those who were mailing checks to the IRS. If you were in Boston, you were at ground zero for one of the scariest moments in recent U.S. history, as a couple of self-made angry young men with homemade bombs created holy havoc near the finish line of the Boston Marathon.

What followed, however, in the manhunt for the bombers was something of a jaw-dropping reality, at least for those who were paying enough attention to see past the raw emotion of the moment. For the first time, we got to see just how far we have come in the way of militarized readiness since the tragedy of 9/11.

At the request of Homeland Security, citizens were "sheltered in place" as the hunt was on for the bombers, who were identified rather quickly through a series of camera images from all angles around the site.

So, a new reality began to set in—that there are a lot of cameras rolling on the average day, on average street corners, in average cities.

Then armored vehicles began to roll through the streets, with heavily armed members of law enforcement going door to door, ready to unleash the power of their weaponry.

Within a matter of days, one of the bombers was dead, and another—his brother—was in custody. And Boston could return to normal. But was there now a new normal? That is, if folks chose to acknowledge it?

In truth, what we saw was just how quickly one of the largest cities in the nation could be closed down and invaded by U.S. forces. That's scary. And it means that somewhere, hidden in the halls of power and justice, plans have been made to accomplish just that.

The occupation went off seamlessly, a marvel of militarized efficiency.

My question—THE question—is: If it had not been done in the shadow of an attack on the city of Boston by (initially) unknown persons, would we tolerate it? Sure, it was easy to let it happen, not knowing if this was the next big terror attack. But, what if it happened in another city, if the threat that prompted it wasn't as immediate as Boston, if the danger was unclear at the moment things were mobilized? What if it wasn't a wannabe Taliban, but Occupy?

The week of April 15, 2013, we saw a page turned in how local, regional, and national law enforcement has evolved in a little more than a decade.

Now we have to decide if it's a good thing. (see Chapter 29 for more on that subject).

Messerism #150

Don't go to the mainstream media to get facts straight from the horse's mouth; what comes out there is usually from the other end.

NINE
MORAL MONDAY: PROTEST DONE RIGHT, TO RIGHT THE RIGHT'S WRONGS

A lot of people voted for Pat McCrory for governor based on his sincere-sounding campaign and his claims to be a reasonable moderate. What no one noticed was the unreasonable people with the checkbooks standing behind him, or—as in the case of Art Pope—above him, working his strings.

A lot of those same people quickly had a case of voter remorse, when it became clear that McCrory was not his own man, and, though he himself might have been moderate, he was not the one in charge of the strings that supported him. And those around him were FAR from moderate.

McCrory was like George W. Bush lite. And Art Pope, who had made—well, inherited—his fortune peddling cheap plastic junk sold in Rose's and his family's other discount chains (think of a poor man's K-Mart, which is already a poor man's Walmart), was the chief marionette, à la Karl Rove, with a dash or two of Koch envy thrown in.

The agenda was clearly a fast-moving, slash-and-burn one. The policies were hard right, and each one followed hard upon the one before. Much of it was downloaded almost word-for-word from the American Legislative Exchange Council (ALEC), a right-wing policy tank (not quite a "think tank" since they don't think, only act). They knew that what they had in store for NC was going to piss people off, so they knew they had to move fast to get it done. After all, it is harder to undo laws than it is to pass them.

The people of NC were shocked, and outraged in large numbers. Including many who had voted for the very villains that now held the metaphoric knives of policy at the public's throat.

It should have been no surprise that there would be protests.

Scott Walker, in Wisconsin, was barely sworn in before the folks showed up in the cold of winter to protest his promised policies. Unfortunately, the cold weather eventually got the best of the crowds. It was Wisconsin, after all.

And Occupy Wall Street was still fresh on many minds. Though with the whole "occupy" sentiment came the difficulty of outlasting the people in those towers of power, who had the law and the ability to wait them out on their side.

What rose up in NC was different, however. And, in being different from these previous protests, this new movement had learned from their mistakes and perfected the notion of protest.

Moral Monday was its name, and it was spearheaded by state NAACP leader Rev. William Barber II, a religious man who called up some striking similarities to another great African American protest leader whom some may recall from the 1960s.

If there's anything the Religious Right hates more than someone actually pointing out what Jesus Christ had to say on a variety of issues that the GOP refuses to support, it's when a black minister is the one doing it. Part of their fear is that the people they dupe into voting for them on somewhat dubious religious grounds might start listening to actual, legitimate Christians who are not just preaching, but practicing, Christian behavior: all the things that the GOP pay cheap lip service to but oppose in reality. And Reverend Barber is just such a charismatic man.

The list of reasons to protest in NC was already long after only a couple of months of full GOP control (as detailed in the last chapter), and it promised to grow longer, the longer they were in control. Something had to be done. Someone had to speak up. Because if these sorts of actions go unquestioned, what's to stop these people from going further, and from assuming that the lack of protest is some form of tacit approval for their draconian methods?

On April 29, 2013, a handful of folks led by Dr. Barber descended on Raleigh to make their protests of the current legislation, and legislators, known. Speeches were made outside the building, and attention was paid, as people started to compare the morals claimed by the GOP, and that same GOP's actions that contradict them.

In a matter of weeks, thousands of people joined the Moral Monday Movement. Weekly they began arriving in Raleigh at 5 p.m. on the dot, to sing, preach, and celebrate unity in opposition to the regime that had taken hold of this state by the throat and were dragging it under.

When all was said and done, and after many GOP leaders were seen fleeing, hiding from the coming protesters, closing their blinds and locking their doors, by the end of the summer of 2013 nearly 1,000 arrests had been made, as Capital Police were instructed to haul off all those people who dared to fill the gallery of the People's House and demand that their voices be heard.

In spite of the arrests, more and more people showed up each and every week, in a peaceful celebration of morals and values, and protest of those in charge who lacked both.

The Moral Monday Movement was a rousing success. After all, it's pretty hard for the folks in charge to effectively bash people of religion, who had wide-ranging support and adoration. Plus, they comported themselves in a peaceable manner, each and every week. No out-of-control, angry mobs, no violent agitators, no groups coming in from other states (all of which the GOP loves to accuse home-grown protesters of being); no, just common citizens of North Carolina looking to be heard by the people governing their own state.

Among the assembled were ministers, teachers, healthcare workers, the elderly, the unemployed, the disenfranchised, and those who simply cared more about improving the big picture than grabbing the big piece of the pie. Closely reflecting the state's population, the protesters were about 30% black, 70% white (NC is 73% white, 22% black, 5% other, according to the 2010 Census).

Of course, the media was shamefully cowed by the prevailing winds of political partisanship.

More photos than not showed only African Americans at the protests. This required some deliberate and tightly cropped editorial manipulation to achieve, since the crowds were massively diverse. (For example, a crowd photo showing several hundred people, mostly white, marching down the street was cropped to show three or four black faces in close-up, with one white person standing behind them.)

I took to spending Tuesdays on my radio show finding all the state media outlets' reports of the actual numbers of people who were at the Moral Monday protests. Typically, the difference varied by several dozen to a few hundred from the actual turnout. Some reports would indicate things like "Nearly 1,000 people protest in state capital," or "hundreds protest," while the actual number was closer to 2,000.

The attempt to manipulate public perception was quite evident, but none more obnoxiously overt than when, in 2014—recounting the total number of Moral Monday protesters arrested the previous year—one news site stated, "More than 930" were arrested. The actual number of arrests was 945. And while true, "more than 930" was a strange way to put it. Why not, "Nearly 950?" Closer to the actual number, and more impressive. Unless of course, the intent of the report is to diminish the significance of the movement.

After the legislative session ended, Moral Mondays took to the road, visiting cities and towns throughout the state, taking the movement local—and thus statewide. Protests were staged from coastal Manteo to Sylva in the far western mountains; in Charlotte, the "Banking Capital of the South" (and Pat McCrory's power base); even in tiny, rural Burnsville, where 500 people turned out, despite strongly conservative, Republican-leaning Yancey County having voted 70% in favor of Amendment One in 2012.

No event was bigger than Asheville's. On August 5, 2013, the week after legislators left Raleigh at the end of their session, "Mountain Moral Monday" brought 8,000 to 10,000 people packing Pack Square Park. It was the single largest of all the Moral Monday protests. More about it in Chapter 13.

And as well-planned, peaceful, and positive in spirit the event was, it was not without some ... tension. Yes, indeed, a villain was in the crowd, trying to snake his way to the microphone.

Tim Moffitt, one of Buncombe County's state representatives, was there on that hot August 5th, and he wanted to speak to the assembled thousands, who would—no doubt—boo him mightily, as he is the most hated man within the city limits.

Want to know why?

Turn to the next chapter, and meet the black-hearted, black-hatted baddie of this book: Little Timmy Moffitt.

Messerism #33

Why do I tend to side with the Democrats? Well, even though they're pretty spineless when it comes to fighting for what they say they believe in, at least they believe in more rights for more people, more freedom for more people, more opportunity for more people. The GOP is all about reducing rights, taking away freedoms, and only siding with those with wealth and influence. Of the two, I would rather support the one with the philosophy of improving the greater good, even if they suck at getting it done ... or even fighting to do so.

TEN
WATER WARS: RALEIGH V. ASHEVILLE

Little Timmy Moffitt

Just like in the days of the Wild West, when the big company came rolling across the Frontier and needed to lay tracks for the railroad or some such thing, and a town stood in their way, they would stop at nothing to drive out the good folks there. Some slick, shystery, Snidely Whiplash-type goon was always behind it. Often, they would send in the big bad dudes to scare the folks, and often they would find a way to cut off the town's water supply as a lever to attempt to push them out.

Well, short of actual big, bad dudes, the NC GOP has plenty of Snidely Whiplash villains on hand. And, as no story of this sort is complete without a Chief Villain, I give you the mustache-twirling, sneering, giggling, baddy: Tim Moffitt. Or as I like to call him: Little Timmy Moffitt.

Sure, there's Governor Pat McCrory, but he's Mortimer Snerd at best. And, though you could Rove your way up Pat's mass of strings to Art Pope, his financier and marionette-in-charge, His Unholiness lacks (and abhors, just like his mentors the Koch brothers) the high-profile, public eye that Moffitt revels in.

No, Little Timmy is the villain of my book, plain and simple. And he not-so-secretly likes it that way.

You see, Timmy is from Asheville—four generations deep. He's the obnoxious kid who never got his hands dirty down on the cattle ranch, and ended up heading off to the big city to become a slick fella who comes back to town to help swindle the good folks he grew up with out of their land and rights—all in the name of progress. Timmy holds more than a bit of a grudge against all those mean people who picked on him for his un-calloused hands, and seemingly lazy work ethic, and total lack of morality. And, having gained power, and the love and backing of the wealthy men from the East, he will prove his devotion to them by destroying those he left behind. And delight in doing so.

Timmy will turn up many times throughout this book. For the record, he is a two-term representative of the 116th House District, which encompasses the south and west of Buncombe County. He's a savvy political campaigner who handily won re-election in 2012, with major aspirations to ascend to the House Speakership, once current Speaker Thom Tillis goes to Washington. (See Chapter 31 for the outcome of those hopes.)

So, the question begs to be asked: Why does Little Timmy hate Asheville so much? As the scion of a multi-generation family here, you would think he has a lot invested in helping to keep Asheville great, safe, clean, healthy, and happy. But, alas, he seems to have a big ax to grind about something—something that is decidedly un-Asheville. Of course, he's not from the city proper: his part of Arden is south of Asheville, and that District encompasses the conservative western part of the county, which sets up a sort of "county-rubes-resent-city-slickers" motif.

In 2013, it became clear that the new, all-powerful regime in Raleigh was going to move fast to do as much damage as possible, as quickly as they could, to all sectors of the population who were not of their particular ilk and pedigree. For their takeover take-down to work, they needed to reduce the opposition—and that opposition's ability to fight them.

You didn't have to be all that bright, or look all that far ahead, to realize that the single biggest threat to their total, unchallenged reign was the city of Asheville. Asheville doesn't suffer as much as more rural parts of the county with mass dysfunction; with built-in gullibility to the nastiest, or stupidest, or craziest assertions—or plain old fearmongering—of the Sarah Palin school of hucksterism; with people who inexplicably vote against their own interests year after year. It does, however, tend to inspire the best in the people who live there (by birth or choice) and to look at progress as a pretty good thing. (Hint: that's why we're called "progressives.") So, Asheville needed to be taken out.

And, much like that stubborn Western town that won't submit to the pressures of the Eastern City Slickers looking to roll over them, Asheville found itself firmly in their sights. And, lo and behold, one of their own, Little Timmy Moffitt, sat high in his saddle as he came riding into town, followed by his new friends and allies, ready to take the town's water supply.

Take the water and run

Among the legislation handed down early by the GOP supremacists in Raleigh was a plan to transfer control of the local water supply from the City of Asheville to "independent" control under the Metropolitan Sewerage District (MSD). Step one to privatization on behalf of Timmy's patrons.

Of course, Timmy, being a "county" boy, not a "city" boy, knew all about the long-running feuds between the city and county over water, feuds that had raged up and quieted down over and over as far back as the 1920s). A lot of folk harbored bitterness and hurt feelings over what was viewed as a strong-arm attempt by the city to control the county through control of the water supply. This conflict even crossed county lines and affected people in neighboring Henderson County.

Timmy's motivations were justified as such: "Taking the system from the city would ensure that water customers outside Asheville would never be charged higher rates than city residents."

The threat had been coming since May 4, 2011, in his first term, when Timmy introduced a bill calling for the seizure of the Asheville water system and transferring it to an MSD authority. Naturally, this met with a huge backlash from elected city officials. So Timmy backed off, taking the whole debate to a "bipartisan" Study Committee—comprised of four Republicans and one Democrat.

They decided to live to fight another day. And that day came in the 2012 election that ushered in complete GOP control of NC. After which, Little Timmy was brave enough to go back to the table, this time, with the support and clout he thought he needed, to finally take the water away from the mean ol' city of Asheville.

The NC House voted, on April 11, 2013, to do just that. House Bill 488 (The Regionalization of Public Utilities) passed 68 to 42, essentially along party lines. Reflecting either utter self-delusion or bottomless cynicism, bill co-sponsor and Timmy cohort (and former Chairman of the Buncombe County Commission) Nathan Ramsey—whose seat also covers rural parts of Buncombe County—claimed on the day of passage that it "is not a partisan measure back home." Ramsey is not quite the same caliber as Timmy, but, as we all know, every chief villain needs a sniveling sidekick.

However, back home, people were in fact plenty mad about it. A nonbinding referendum in the 2012 election, when the water transfer was proposed, saw 86% of the voters come out against it. And Asheville City Council voted unanimously to file a lawsuit against the state to stop them.

Even elder statesman of the WNC GOP, former Congressman Charles ("Chainsaw Charlie") Taylor, came out publicly against the GOP's plan.

But on May 14, Pope Art jerked Puppet Pat's strings, and it became law.

Punch. Counterpunch. Punch.

Six days later, on May 20, the City of Asheville asked NC Superior Court Judge Harold Manning, Jr. for an injunction preventing H488 from taking effect.

Then it got ugly.

Determined to get their way, even if 86% of the people were against them, Moffitt, Ramsey, and Henderson County's Chuck McGrady began trying to pressure City Council to drop its lawsuit. The first wave of threats was that the upcoming off-year City Council elections could be altered by the powers that be in the state. In NC, you see, municipal charters are "creatures" of the legislature, so the Lege can do whatever it likes to screw a city.

Then a provision in the previous H94 law suddenly reared its head, as the folks living in Greenville, in the eastern part of the state, discovered that a provision in that law applies to H488—which could mean that other towns and cities were now subject to, and vulnerable to, the same kind of state-mandated takeover Asheville was facing. This did not sit well. And it caused a bit of an uproar among the Moffitt Mafia.

Which led to—on July 2, 2013—the entire NC Senate having to vote to remove the line from H94 that was giving everyone such pause. And without that particular line in H94, the constitutionality of the seizure of Asheville's water was now in question—in a major way.

On September, 6, the injunction that Asheville wanted was granted by Judge Manning, who emerged as quite an interesting character in the whole affair. He openly mocked some of the Republican legislature's approach to legislating, and the general knuckleheadedness of their attempts to take Asheville's water while first pretending it wasn't a grudge match against Asheville and then, when caught lying about it after Greenville expressed their concerns, deliberately changing the law so it specifically targeted Asheville alone. Which is one of the things that made the law unconstitutional in the first place! (Laws that affect only a single jurisdiction are not allowed in NC except under very specific circumstances.)

On June 9, 2014, Asheville won its lawsuit.

In typical villain fashion, Little Timmy's response to the ruling was that he was "somewhat amused" that NC cities even had the authority to sue the state government. No word on whether or not he was twirling his mustache (well, his carefully "unkempt" five-o'clock shadow) at the time. And, also, no word as to whether or not he then went to try and find a young damsel to tie to train tracks.

But he was totally upfront about his desire for the state to appeal. Which it did.

Before that, though, on June 10—the day after the ruling, and still in his temper-tantrum stage—Timmy came up with a new threat: to abolish the Buncombe County Culture and Recreation Authority, which the legislature had directed the county to establish just the previous year as a way to keep the city from benefiting from the county's parks and recreation facilities and functions.

And then Timmy got caught on tape admitting that the move to exclude Asheville from the county-wide CRA was specifically in retribution for the city's successful lawsuit; he cited the lawsuit and said that until it was settled, he wanted to make sure Asheville didn't benefit from it.

He also made some remarks that should scare other towns and cities:

"The way we constructed the bill was the appropriate way. We constructed the bill as we felt was necessary to get it enacted into law, in order to put together a framework that provides for the regionalization of water and sewer utilities, not only in our area, but in other areas throughout the state. So it's a framework that's in place, involuntary when it comes to Asheville's standpoint, but certainly can be voluntary throughout the rest of the state, or in certain situations, equally as involuntary." [sic]

The appeal will be presented by NC Attorney General Roy Cooper, who is the leading elected Democrat in state government and a viable challenger to Pat McCrory in 2016. It was a bit of a head-scratcher that Cooper would actually fight to overturn Asheville's victory. He says he has no choice as the state's attorney but to defend the state's actions—kind of like a defense attorney who has to defend a murderer he knows is guilty. We can only hope his heart won't be in it, as winning the appeal would certainly give him a black eye among the progressive stronghold that is Asheville.

A curious wrinkle emerged in light of the appeal, and the participation of Cooper, thanks to the NC House Finance Committee, which asserted that a "stay" could be issued, pending the final outcome of the appeal(s), which would allow for the state to go ahead with the water system transfer to an independent authority, which could go into effect sooner than later, and make it so that Asheville would lose its water while waiting for all appeals to play out. After which, it would be almost impossible to get it back, even if the final appeal was in favor of Asheville's position. All that, in spite of having won their lawsuit.

Scumbags in charge, and we're living under scumbag rules. They have such unchallenged control in NC now that even when they lose, they've manipulated things so that they actually can still get their way.

No heroes riding off into the sunset yet, and Little Timmy and his posse of black hats are still sitting up on the ridge, staring down on Asheville, with sneering glee.

Climate change update, Asheville bureau

Speaking of water ...

By July 1, 2013, the Western NC Region had reached, and surpassed, its average annual rainfall. One of the wettest summers on record led to massive flooding in low-lying areas, and a number of mudslides.

But, no—oh, no, no—there's no climate change going on here. Keep moving! Nothing to see here!

Messerism #42

Isn't it ironic that all the same people who say they don't believe in evolution seem to also be the ones who spent a lot of their time worrying over the rotted corpses of dinosaurs?

ELEVEN
A Few Local Heroes? Check!

Of course, now that you've met the proper villain of the book, you're probably asking yourself, "Are there any heroes?"

There are plenty of great heroes on the front lines in NC, fighting for what's good, just and right, in spite of the morally questionable and politically corrupted elements that have seized the state.

Time to meet some of the good guys:

Barry Summers

I had never met, nor heard of, Barry before getting my radio show gig. But once I got to know him, he became a fast friend, and one of my favorite guests.

Barry does it old-school. He is the human burr in the saddle of the folks who are trying to get away with some pretty dastardly things in North Carolina. He stays better informed on the slippery nuances of those who think they are being politically savvy than anyone I know.

The main focus for Barry, however, is issues relating to the water system in Asheville. You can find Barry, and his constant updates on water issues, and many other issues, on the website: www.saveourwaterwnc.com.

No one followed the state's attempts to steal, and ultimately privatize, the Asheville water system more closely than Barry. When Little Timmy Moffitt sees him coming, I'm sure he thinks about turning and heading in the other direction. And in the state capital, Barry's face is well known by many of our local, regional, and state politicians.

Beyond water issues, Barry was the only member of the public to show up for a hearing on bringing the drone industry into North Carolina. That one nearly slipped in under everyone's radar—but not

Barry's. And, much to his own shock, he discovered that taking on the issue of drones in the skies of NC gained him favorable conversation in Tea Party circles of all places! (More on drones later.)

Barry has also found himself on the official speakers' list for both Mountain Moral Monday rallies in Asheville, having earned a stellar reputation and proven to know his stuff better than anyone else around.

He's also a force to be reckoned with, and holds a special place in my heart, for being one of the two gentlemen who helped turn an interloping Timmy Moffitt away from the stage at the first Mountain Moral Monday. Timmy thought he should come up and speak to the assembled crowd, despite being the least popular man in town. Clearly, some misaligned ego issues. A group of ladies calling themselves the "Green Grannies" cut off Timmy's dash toward the microphone, and then Barry, along with my next hero, headed him off at the pass and ushered him off the stage and into the waiting hands of an angry mob of educators, who recorded their interaction with him and later published it online. (As did my publisher, who wrote up an interview with him for Asheville's black-owned multicultural monthly, *The Urban News*.)

Cecil Bothwell

Asheville City Council has many great people on it, who help keep Asheville great through their steady-handed ways, and strong moral compass. Bothwell is one of the finest examples of what makes Asheville great.

He's one of the only people who could end up on the annual Best of WNC polls (as conducted by the *Mountain Xpress* weekly newspaper (for which he was once an award-winning investigative reporter) in both the local "Hero" and "Villain" categories. He is a somewhat polarizing fella. Why? Probably because of his unapologetic manner. He has his convictions, and he won't blink when challenged. And that can inspire as much as it rubs some folks the wrong way.

He's also extremely upfront about his views on many things, and is an admitted atheist ("post-theist" is his own word for it). Which can certainly cause some folks to bristle.

Moreover, he is a staunch supporter of the environment, and he's been instrumental in a number of initiatives that have helped make Asheville, greener, safer, healthier, and happier. Without his leadership, and his stubborn resolve, Asheville might not be the great place it is today.

Gordon Smith

Another Asheville City Council member, one with a heart and soul bigger than most people I know. He is a successful therapist who got into local politics after being a highly regarded contributor to the Scrutiny Hooligans website, because he felt he could help make a positive difference in the growth of Asheville. Issues like a living wage, food safety, and decent housing opportunities for low-income individuals prove that Smith is more about humanity than politics.

I can speak to his integrity from a personal standpoint, as he was the therapist my son saw during our post-divorce adjustment period, and during a period of time when my son was having struggles in school, which I felt were related to the new family alignments happening around him at the time. We took him to Gordon for several months, and found great resolution on many fronts. It was a wonderful service by a true professional with a big heart.

During the middle of the therapy sessions, I got my gig on radio. Knowing that Gordon was a City Council member running for re-election, I offered to let him come on the show to talk about his campaign. I reached out via email, and he responded that, as he had entered a professional arrangement with me in his role as a therapist, he would not come on the show. This was in spite of the clear benefit of having his message go out over the airwaves.

He was simply too ethical, and too much of a professional, to cross those lines. When pressed, he said that if both my ex-wife and I were to officially end that relationship, then and only then would he come on the radio show.

Since this all took place a couple of months after the last session, I had assumed that we had cut those ties, but Gordon wanted it to be official. So, after an exchange of emails among all of us—ex-wife, me, Gordon—we ended our patient-therapist relationship, and he felt free to be a guest on the show.

As you might have guessed, I was impressed by his professionalism and integrity. Gordon won and continues to serve the city of Asheville proudly.

Ellen Frost

In the 2012 election, some of the legislature's crafty redistricting came into play just outside of Asheville, on the campus of Warren-Wilson College. Students who had voted in the previous election in the convenient, well-known location nearest campus did their patriotic duty and showed up there again to cast their ballots. However, since district lines had been moved, some of them inadvertently voted in the wrong place.

Chaos ensued when the race ended up being very close for one Buncombe County Commissioner seat. "Too close to call" got a whole new meaning for voters in Buncombe County.

Lawsuits, recounts, threats of more lawsuits followed. When the smoke cleared, Ellen Frost won by a mere eighteen votes. And thus, the balance of the County Commissioners Board was tipped to four Democrats and three Republicans. As narrow as you could imagine. (The County Commission had had five members elected county-wide until the legislature, in 2011, divided it into three districts and increased it to seven members as a way to turn it Republican. It almost worked.)

In the spring on 2013, the Commissioners voted along party lines to pass benefits for same-sex couples who work for the County. This was a major leap forward in the state that had passed Amendment One, double-banning gay marriage, less than a year earlier.

Had Frost not won that seat by eighteen votes, it would not have passed. Every vote does count.

Leni Sitnick

A former Mayor of Asheville, Sitnick is one of my personal Asheville heroes. It was her leadership in the late 1990s that helped to broaden the appeal and freshen the brand of Asheville, which led to it becoming the famously infamous city that many people know it to be today.

In 2002, back when I was running Area: 45, my small theater and arts incubator space downtown, I met her in person, thanks to her daughter being a regular visitor and a fan of the OxyMoron Improv Comedy night that we hosted. Leni was in the audience one night, laughing a little too hard at some slightly off-color comedy, which only got funnier when I pointed her out to the audience. She laughed even harder.

During Mountain Moral Monday, she agreed to come on my radio show for an interview. It was the first time I really got to chat with her and give her the proper credit and respect for all she had done to make Asheville great. She was gracious, and quite humble.

I'm also quite proud that she finally called in to the show one day in early 2014. It was the first time she called, but just knowing that she was out there listening was a tremendous support boost for me personally.

Brian Turner

Turner is the man who took on Timmy Moffitt head to head, engaging in a *mano-a-mano* showdown for State House seat #116. And, while there's nothing especially new about a politician facing a challenger, there are some wrinkles here worth taking the satirical iron to.

In the plus column, Brian Turner is not a politician. He decided to run out of concern for the state and a strong need to get Timmy Moffitt back into the private sector ASAP. Little Timmy's ambitions never stopped with keeping his House seat, but have always aimed at the House Speakership which Thom Tillis (more on him later) was glad to vacate in pursuit of Kay Haygan's U.S. Senate seat (see Chapter 31). Timmy also has some sweet pals over on the American Legislative Exchange Council (ALEC), and has always shown more interest in serving his own needs than those of his constituents.

In fact, his ambitions are so precious to him that he felt it was unfair that anyone was planning to challenge him; the last thing he expected was to actually have to run for his seat again, rather than just keep it and ascend to a higher platform.

So, when Brian Turner filed to run against him, Timmy had a tantrum. A meeting was arranged between the two, facilitated by old-fashioned, fairly traditional moderate Republican County Commissioner David King (who lost his 2014 re-election primary to an unknown Tea Party-leaning upstart who accused him of—horrors—"working with" the majority Democrats on the Commision). Turner left the meeting feeling as if he had perhaps been offered an implicit bribe to drop out of the race, and then more than a thinly veiled threat from the moneyed right when he declined to bow out.

A state-appointed ethics board eventually cleared Moffitt of wrongdoing, after Turner made a case of it. Though the investigation led by a Republican-run Board of Elections was a bit like a panel of foxes finding the henhouse bandit not guilty, despite the feathers in the fox's mouth.

Then Turner pulled ahead of Moffitt in polling, showing an early and consistent lead of at least two points.

Of course, a dirty politician will fight dirty. As will those who support him.

Home video of an old man walking down an Asheville street uprooting Turner yard signs, then tossing them down so that no one can see them as they drive by, emerged in the summer of 2014. The video was shot on a smartphone from an upstairs window—by the person who put the signs up and wanted to catch whoever was knocking them over.

Complaints also started pouring in about "outside money"—from downtown-Asheville supporters who seemed to be the majority of Turner's donors. Meanwhile, Moffitt's own donor base was skewed heavily toward big-money out-of-state donors—like fellow ALEC supporters.

Regardless of where the money came from, Turner was out-raising Moffitt—and beating him at a game the GOP thinks they should be allowed to play while denying their opponents the same courtesy. (Then, naturally, they whine when they start losing.)

One indication of Turner's success was that his second-quarter fundraising, from more than 700 individual donors, widely surpassed Moffitt's, who got money from nine (yes, 9) individuals. Turner took in no donations from Political Action Committees or big-money type donors, while 81% of Moffitt's funds originated with those types of organizations and people.

Drew Reisinger

Young (under 30) and a non-career politician, Drew Reisinger was appointed Buncombe County Register of Deeds when his long-time predecessor retired. It's not the sexiest of offices to run for, win, and occupy, but he won a full term in the 2012 election. Reisinger set the tone for his tenure in the summer of 2013 when he announced that he would accept applications for same-sex couples seeking marriage licenses. His theory was that equality would eventually come to pass, even in the Tar Heel State, and he wanted Buncombe County to be at the forefront of welcoming same-sex marriage. More on that in a moment.

But in the summer of 2014, controversy erupted when the Buncombe County Commissioners blamed Reisinger for choosing safety over expediency the previous winter.

The "problem" started during one of those Polar Vortex weather events. A massive snowstorm was setting in on February 12, so Reisinger closed his office early and sent his staff of seventeen full-time employees home. The snow set in, and the next morning, with almost eight inches on the ground, he kept the office closed. Which led to a major political SNAFU.

Because Buncombe County offices don't close for bad weather. Just like the Postal Service, WE NEVER CLOSE! Rah-rah-rah!! And Reisinger didn't have the authority to shut his office. Because, after all, some folks might be so eager to get to the Register of Deeds office that they would risk life, limb, and a totaled car to get there during a major snowstorm.

And don't mistake me because we're in the South, and don't know jack about real snowstorms. And don't point to those wild social-media memes of Imperial Walkers and Echo Base from *The Empire Strikes Back* that were Photoshopped into scenes of Atlanta's traffic jam that winter, when a lot of folks got stranded in a little snow and ice, due to public officials miscalculating when and how to send people home.

Of course, a week later, another big storm hit NC, and places like Raleigh (where they truly don't typically get snow) replaced Atlanta in the Ice Planet Hoth Photoshop memes.

Sorry. We're in the mountains, and we know snow!

Jeff Messer

But sure enough, that summer, when the County Manager and the Commission were planning the new budget, some conservative political activists complained that the Register of Deeds had given his employees an unauthorized "vacation." So the commissioners wrung their collective hands, and with the infinite wisdom of a public board facing an election, they decided that, instead of simply asking those seventeen employees to give up a day and a half of personal or sick time, every single county employee should be paid the equivalent of an extra day-and-a-half's salary. One year before, these same Buncombe County Commissioners had, admirably, offered all employees equal benefits for same-sex partners; this time they made the knucklehead play of the year by allocating nearly half a million dollars to "compensate" all county employees. That way, they could penalize the Register of Deeds, and dump the problem on the taxpayers, and be seen as ... tough? ... responsible? ... dumb? Or just invulnerable to criticism from the rabid right.

Needless to say, both sides of the political spectrum instead let out a collective "WTF?" (Who says we can't find common ground?) And, as this book goes to press, those "conservative activists" have launched a lawsuit against Reisinger's "public official bond" asking half a million dollars in damages. Of course, they really want him to pay it personally, but they'll settle for extorting yet more money from the taxpayers.

Reisinger had raised hackles by being one of the only Registers of Deeds in the state to allow same-sex couples to register for marriage licenses. Under Amendment One he was prohibited from *issuing* such licenses, but he wanted to make sure that couples who wanted to fill out the paperwork and *register* for marriage could do so.

And, on October, 10 2014, U.S. District Court Judge Max O. Cogburn Jr. vindicated his position, ruling in Asheville that, in accordance with the earlier decision by the Fourth Circuit Court of Appeals, the Amendment One prohibition against same-sex marriage was unconstitutional. So Reisinger kept the office open past 5 p.m.—maybe to make up for those wasted "vacation" hours—and issued marriage licenses to several Ashevlle couples, who were promptly married by Rev. Lisa Bovee-Kemper of the Unitaran Universalist Congregation of Asheville. Rev. Lisa, it should be noted, was the host and emcee of the second Mountain Moral Monday held in August—more on that in Chapter 29.

Oh, that Drew Reisinger, making waves and raising hackles and spicing up the Tea Party chai at every turn.

Mike Mason

In April, 2013, Tampa TV news reporter Mike Mason came to town. Among the first in-depth stories he got interested in was an ongoing tale from south Asheville about a nearly 30-year-old chemical plant site that had been linked to poisoning the ground water of a nearby community. The story of the CTS scandal and the EPA's decades-long inaction on it has grown bigger and bigger every year.

Tate MacQueen

Mason described Tate McQueen as "Asheville's Erin Brokovich" for his efforts to expose the truth about the groundwater contamination left behind by CTS Corporation and find solutions for residents of his community. MacQueen, a public-school history teacher and soccer coach, is one of the most honest and forthright people I've ever met. You don't often meet somebody you'd describe as having unwavering dignity and nobility, but he does; the more I've gotten to know him, the more I like him.

After years of struggling to dig out the truth, and of being roundly ignored by elected officials and the EPA, MacQueen got fed up enough to decide to run for the 10th District seat in the U.S. House of Representatives, currently held by GOP lackey Patrick McHenry. I was lucky enough to be in on this bit of news for a couple of months before it went public.

Tate is the first to offer credit to others for the strides made in exposing the CTS contamination, but he stands out as the clear leader of the pack. And a charismatic leader he is. He sincerely cares about his community and his fellow human beings, and his honesty and integrity must be scary to those who peddle the politics of fear and intimidation. More than once, his opponents tried pushing back, even trying to make an issue of his phone-in updates on my radio show during the school year: they claimed

Jeff Messer

he was making radio appearances on school time. (Note: My show starts at 3 p.m., after school lets out, and typically Tate would call in during the 5 o'clock hour.) Clearly he was ruffling some sensitive feathers, a clear sign that he was on the right track.

As a teacher who understands the needs of education, it should have come as no surprise that, when it came time to find and unveil a tour bus for his campaign, MacQueen found and retrofitted an old yellow school bus. The bus, purchased locally and retrofitted to use bio-diesel, is replete with a whistle-stop-style stage build onto the back that's accessed through the old emergency door.

Unlike his opponent, MacQueen spent every moment of his free time (during the school year), and all his time in the summer (after officially stepping down as an educator), on the road, visiting all seven counties in the district. There isn't a person he won't stop to talk to, no matter their party affiliation, and there's not conversation that he shies away from. His honesty and forthright approach became startlingly refreshing to many people who had yet to see, meet or even speak to Patrick McHenry—one of the most absent representatives of his home district in memory.

As a campaigner, Tate MacQueen could give Jimmy Stewart a run for his money.

In the spring of 2014 *Mother Jones* magazine listed the states that had the most severe gerrymandering, and how that would affect elections for Congress. The most startling number on the list went to to North Carolina, where it now takes approximately 3.2 blue votes to counteract every red vote and get a Democrat elected.

No other state was so severely skewed. Only one state on the list skewed toward the Blue over the Red: Illinois. You know, land of Obama, dirty politics, etc. Oh, yeah. And Lincoln.

Even faced with that daunting statistic, MacQueen was undeterred, and unceasingly criss-crossed the district in his souped-up school bus, shaking as many hands, and talking to as many people as possible, and showing what it looks like to actually care about what he says, and whom he's saying it to.

Integrity is typically seen as a liability in politics these days. Legitimate integrity, at any rate. Sure, they will all talk about it, and pretend to have it, but no one really believes it anymore, despite the political smile and lapel-pin flag. We expect to be lied to by politicians. We expect lip service. What we don't expect is someone who actually means what he says, and proves it.

And that's Tate MacQueen. The real deal. In a way he's better than we deserve, in this age of jaded, mangled politics; but he's sure what real democracy needs.

Honorable mentions

- Buncombe County District Court Judge Ed Clontz, a soft-spoken, fair-minded judicial champion;
- Leslie Boyd, Moral Monday mover and shaker, as well as the heartbeat of WNC Health Advocates;
- Roy Cooper, NC Attorney General, the highest-ranking elected Democrat in the state;
- Katie Damien, local filmmaker whose documentary *My Toxic Backyard* brought perspective and focus to the contamination site in South Asheville; and
- the late Laurie Masterton, founder of regionally trendsetting and nationally famous Laurey's Catering. RIP to this wonderful woman and community icon, both for her personal fight against cancer, and her fight for others, and her huge impact on inspiring others to new heights of public service. She was one of the most amazing people I ever got to interview on my radio show.

Messerism #27

I wonder if the right wing feels sympathy for the Empire when they watch Star Wars, *or for the Sheriff of Nottingham when they watch* Robin Hood? *Or do they actually think, somewhere deep down, that it's the good guys they identify with?*

TWELVE
FOR EVERY SUPER-HERO FRIEND, THERE HAS TO BE A LEGION OF DOOM.

Of course, little Timmy Moffitt can't carry all of the villainy of this story by himself. His saddlebags just aren't that big, and the horse he rode in on can't bear such a heavy load.

You've met some heroes. Now let me introduce the major villains:

Thom Tillis

Blind ambition. Remember John Dean's book of that name about Richard Nixon's White House? Just like those guys, Thommy Tillis isn't satisfied to be just Speaker of NC's House. He wants to be in the U.S. Senate. He wants it so bad he couldn't even be bothered to stick around for the budget talks that overran the legislative session of 2014, because it cuts into his ability to campaign for his grail.

A member of the General Assembly since 2006, Tillis achieved his dream of finding a dandy step-stool for higher office, and dandier paychecks from ever-deeper-pocketed patrons, when he gained the Speaker's gavel as part of the GOP takeover.

Like Timmy Moffitt he's a member of ALEC, and he's accomplished a number of head-smack-inducing moments. Highlights include:
- Giggling derisively, along with his fellow debaters, in a GOP debate ahead of the 2014 primary, when the subject of climate change came up
- Teaming up with State Senate Leader Phil Berger in the spring of 2014 to release a highly questionable finding of potential voter fraud in NC that, if proven true, would be the biggest voter fraud scandal in the entire history of the world (more on that later)

- Accidentally telling the truth—the crème de la crème of Thom's numbskullery—when answering a question about African American and Latino voters in NC: he told the Carolina Business Review that the "traditional [read "white"] population of North Carolina is more or less stable. It's not growing."
- "Leading" the 2014 short session of the General Assembly, which led to major disagreement between the House and Senate over the budget and teacher's pay. When the two houses could not come to terms, things ran over. Five weeks over. To the tune of an extra $1,000,000 to the taxpayers. And where was Thom? Out fund-raising for his Senate race against Kay Hagan. In Washington, DC. Somebody leaked a photo of him kicked back at Reagan Airport listening to his iPod.

Patrick McHenry

Ah, little Mac. Or, "Little Mc." McHenry is the incumbent that Tate MacQueen is looking to unseat. Not only does Tate have the "a" in his Mac, but he also has spent more time in District 10 than McHenry, who has yet to visit the CTS contamination site or the community affected by it.

McHenry has been a Representative since 2005, when he was the youngest member of the 110th Congress, elected at age 33. Before that he was in the NC House.

Before that, he was working for Karl Rove in 2000 as the National Coalition Director for George W. Bush's campaign.

Little Mc has had a hard time focusing on his district in NC, but he has spent time ruffling plenty of feathers, with his sometimes immature tendencies to mouth off like a frat-house prankster bragging about setting fire to the bag of dog shit on the little old lady's front porch.

During the Bush war years he spent some time partying it up in Iraq. And when he was turned away from the gym because he lacked proper credentials, he got in hot water for referring to one of Dick Cheney's highly-paid, Haliburtonian contractors as "a two-bit security guard."

Little Mc pitched a hissy fit and demanded to see the guard's superior, who didn't take to kindly to Mc's attitude, and escorted him back to his room.

While rolling around Baghdad, McHenry also got in trouble for riding around and gleefully pointing out—on videotape— all sorts of destruction and landmarks our forces had messed up. When they saw the video, Veteran's blog *VetVoice* pointed out that McHenry's video violated operational security by showing things that the enemy could use to their advantage. The Pentagon asked him to remove the video.

Now 41, but not much more responsible or accomplished, McHenry clearly prefers to spend time anywhere but North Carolina's 10th District, where most people couldn't pick him out of a line-up.

Mark Meadows

Shutdown shakedown clown Mark Meadows came to power in 2012, getting elected to the U.S. House of Representatives from North Carolina's 11th District, succeding Blue Dog Democrat Heath Shuler.

His major distinction, so far, has been authoring the angry letter that led to the October 2013 government shutdown in an attempt to stop the Affordable Care Act. Not only did his epic ignorance lead him to this folly, which had no effect on the launch of the ACA but cost his constituents back home over a million dollars a day in lost economic activity during the busiest tourism month of the year.

Also worthy of note: The Meadows shutdown also ended up being an affront on the Second Amendment, since the Bureau of Alcohol, Tobacco, and Firearms had to stop issuing new gun permits.

Meadows also made a chest-pounding display in a Congressional hearing with the EPA, in the shadow of a Supreme Court ruling concerning a toxic emergency near Meadows's district. He asked a lot of applause-worthy questions and cited the problems back home. He seemed pretty tough, and very concerned. Unfortunately for people who truly cared, the person he was "standing up to" had nothing to do with that particular region, and had no way of answering the Congressman's questions or addressing residents' concerns.

Jeff Messer

Phil Berger

First elected in 2000, Berger became the State Senate Minority Leader in 2004, then in 2010 was chosen Senate President Pro Tem. That made him the first Republican in that role since the late 19th century. (And, no, that's not a typo.)

Berger briefly earned a bit of respect in June of 2014 for being the only Republican member of the General Assembly to actually sit down and have a discussion with Moral Monday protesters who were outside his office. Then he blew it: within minutes of their departure he let it be known he was planning to totally ignore their concerns.

If anything really sets Berger apart from his more run-of-the-mill GOP colleagues, it's the stunning April 2014 joint statement he issued with Speaker Thom, declaring he had an alarmingly high series of numbers showing evidence of massive North Carolina voter fraud. (See more on that in Chapter 21.)

Art Pope

The Koch brother from another mother, writ somewhat smaller—though don't tell him so, because he thinks pretty highly of himself—is the man with the strings manipulating the Pat McCrory marionette.

Pope got rich as a retail store owner. Well, actually, he got rich as the heir of a retail store owner. Then he got richer than his rich dad, so he can claim to be a "self-made" man. The Pope family empire is made up of those little Dollar Store-type places where only the poorest of poor can afford to shop. And he's made a lot of money selling cheap merchandise to the poor at almost cheap prices. When McCrory appointed him—let me rephrase that. When he instructed McCrory to appoint him NC's Budget Director, he started right away to increase his shopper base by making more and more people in the state poor.

Pope spends vast amounts of his wealth to control state government and, therefore, the state itself. In the mid-2000s, he helped two groups, Americans For Prosperity and the Civitas Institute, open shop in NC. He spent $1.5 million on the 2010 and 2012 campaigns to usher in right-wing control in the state. The 2010 elections were especially important to him, because the Republican majority he bought that year got to redistrict the entire state (following the Obama plot to hold a Census). That ensured them an even bigger Republican majority in 2012—and for the rest of the decade.

Back in 1990, Pope was a co-founder of the John Locke Foundation, and for several years he was a state representative during the long era of Democratic governance. He finally realized that his money talking was more effective than his political walking.

As of 2014, Pope, through his family foundation, has spent more than $108,000,000 on public policy in the past quarter century. Roughly half that amount went to create a number of conservative groups: John Locke Foundation ($30 million), The Civitas Institute ($11.6 million), Americans for Prosperity ($5 million), The Pope Center for Education Policy ($4.5 million), and the Institute for Constitutional Law ($4.5 million).

A number of the GOP General Assembly measures that passed in 2013 were spearheaded by Pope and/or one or more of his massively funded groups. Among them, the Assembly:

- blocked Medicaid expansion
- restricted access to abortion
- slashed unemployment benefits
- lowered personal and corporate tax rates
- funded private and religious school vouchers
- enacted the most extreme voter ID laws in the nation
- ended public financing of judicial elections
- repealed the Racial Justice Act that had begun freeing wrongfully-convicted innocent inmates

Although he doesn't state it in his official biographrical sketches, Art Pope's ambition is to grow up to be a Koch. He's working overtime to get there.

Renee Ellmers

Ellmers is a member of the U.S. Congress. And a Republican. That should tell you all you need to know, but there's more. Think of her as a mating of Sarah Palin's greed with Michelle Bachman's looniness—but without those genteel ladies' character. Sort of like being Dubya, but not as smart.

Think I'm being too harsh?

Here are just two of her note-worthy ditzy doozies:

When the Mark Meadows shutdown was underway, and pressure was on for political folk to either talk tough against it, or to try and justify it, Ellmers kept it real. She was asked about her own pay as a CongressGOPer, since all government employees and millions of private-sector workers were not getting paid during the shutdown. She asserted (with no shame), "I need my paycheck. That's the bottom line. I understand that there may be some other members who are deferring their paychecks, and I think that's admirable. I'm not in that position."

No, she's not in a position to be admirable. On any level. Not only was she totally unconcerned about the nearly one million federal employees who got furloughed during the shutdown and needed *their* paychecks; when attempts were brought up to allow a clean "continuing resolution"—no budget or legislative changes allowed—so as to reopen the government, Renee, along with the entire House Republican Caucus, voted against even bringing the legislation to the floor.

Then, just when she'd been out of the news long enough for everybody to stop paying attention to her, she found a way to say something even more stupid. In the summer of 2014, she participated in a panel discussion on "Women and the Republican Party," which is more and more an oxymoron anyway. But, (since she is one), while "thinking" out loud in response to a question about how the Congress should address the federal budget, she said this:

"Men do tend to talk about things on a much higher level. Many of my male colleagues, when they go to the House floor, you know, they've got some pie chart, or graph behind them, and they're talking about trillions of dollars, and how, you know, the debt is awful and, you know, we all agree with that.... We need our male colleagues to understand that if you can bring it down to a woman's level and what everything that she is balancing in her life—that's the way to go."

Apparently Renee can't balance much of anything. Can't balance her checkbook without a huge, unearned government paycheck; can't balance a pie chart (probably wants to know if it's apple or peach); and clearly can't balance the responsibilities of a Congressman. She went on to note, in the same panel discussion, that what women most want is more time, including "more time in the morning to get ready."

No, Renee Ellmers is no Sarah Palin, but she's working hard to be a kind of training-bra version for NC. So much so that when cornered about the quotes she insisted that she had been taken out of context and blamed "gotcha journalism."

Before being elected as part of the Tea Party's 2010 mad dash to power, Ellmers was a registered nurse. Once there, she voted against the Violence Against Women Reauthorization Act of 2013 and vocally opposed abortion rights. (Miranda deBruhl, the TeaBagger who defeated County Commissioner David King in his Republican primary race, is also a nurse; maybe *they* are what's wrong with American healthcare!)

Clearly, Renee Ellmers doesn't have a very high opinion of women's brains or ability; she understands that the gals just won't get it unless men "bring it down to a woman's level." I guess she's the pudding that is the proof.

Michelle Presnell

Loco local yokel Michelle Presnell is another state representative, one who comes to Raleigh by way of my beloved small town of Burnsville. So it pains me that she made big news in 2013 for some of the most ignorant remarks of the year.

I was shocked to get an email from a Burnsville friend, just before this story broke out and became a national bit of news, in which my friend shared his email exchange with Presnell.

It started with the ACLU moving to stop Rowan County from opening their local meetings with an official Christian prayer. Local people complained, and soon enough—surprise, surprise—along came House Resolution (HR) 494 which stated that North Carolina may establish a state religion (want to guess which one?). Presnell's fingerprints were all over this upstart proposal, which she cosponsored and which later evaporated under the scrutiny.

My friend emailed Presnell, as a concerned citizen asking for clarification. It went like this (some editing has occurred to streamline the conversation, though all of Presnell's replies are whole and intact):

Jeff Messer

> Dear Michele Presnell:
> ... I strongly oppose the idea of declaring a State Religion. I believe it violates our country's constitution and freedom of religion is one of America's founding principles. I hope you reconsider your position on this as you represent our area. I believe it will be divisive among North Carolinians and that is not something I would be proud of my representatives for instigating and institutionalizing.

Presnell's reply (verbatim):

> "Where did you get that??? State religion??? Do you even know why this legislation is coming to the legislators? The famed ACLU is telling Rowan County they may not pray before Commissioner Meetings. We pray in Raleigh before our legislative meetings, US Congress prays in Washington DC, why can they not pray?"

You'll notice, as I did, that immediately after expressing shock at the very idea of establishing a state religion, she launches into a series of justifications for doing exactly that.

So my friend wrote her back.

> Dear Michele Presnell,
> I appreciate your response. Yes, I do understand that the ACLU is suing Rowan County and I think they have clearly articulated why they are not comfortable with prayer before Commissioners Meetings. I wanted you, as my Representative, to know that I do not think the proposed bill is a good solution to that problem – I think it would cause additional problems. Would you be comfortable with a public prayer to Allah before a legislative meeting in Raleigh?

Presnell's reply (verbatim):

> "No, I do not condone terrorism. We just need to start taking a stand on our religious freedom or it will be whisked away from us."

Apparently, Michele Presnell thinks that praying to Allah is equal to terrorism—and that "our" religious freedom belongs only to her fellow Christians. Ignorant? Sure.

So, next from my friend:

> Dear Michele Presnell,
> I am saddened that you make a leap from Allah to terrorism so quickly. My point about asking if you personally would be comfortable with a prayer to Allah is precisely why we do need to take a stand for religious freedom. Your response seems to indicate that you are not comfortable having a state or a state representative honoring a religion other than your own. So you seem to be saying that you yourself are not comfortable with the fundamental premise of the bill. What the bill proposes does whisk away religious freedom. If the state sets a precedent of choosing one religion above others, we have to be prepared for any religion to be chosen as the preferential one.
>
> Thank you for considering this,

A well-thought-out reply from my friend, would you not agree? Certainly, with such a solid argument, Presnell must be able to see the perspective. Right?

Presnell's reply (verbatim):

> "No, you are wrong. Have a good day."

That's it! That's Burnsville's state representative—not the brightest candle in that chandelier. Did she know she could not win, or she was simply too self-deluded to realize that she looked almost as foolish as she did ignorant and unprofessional?

My friend, Britt Kaufmann, emailed me this entire conversation, and of course, with my jaw down on the floor, I quickly broke the story on my radio show. Meanwhile, Britt had sent it to the Raleigh newspaper, which ran with it, and then it was picked up by national media.

I sure was proud to have the story first. Right here, in little ol'

Jeff Messer

Asheville, with my weak-ass AM radio signal. I guess some things are just so juicy, there's no way they don't get out, and travel fast.

And that's a partial, but significant list of some of the true villains who are in power in—and over—the wonderful state of North Carolina.

THIRTEEN
MORAL MONDAYS HIT THE ROAD

Mountain Moral Monday rolls into town

August 5, 2013. My day started with a call in to The Bill Press Show, where I gave his national audience a taste of what was happening in Asheville and across the state. I had been on Bill's show once before, giving some local perspective on the state movement when it launched, but now it was in my town, and it was looking to be a new page, as this was the first event to be held outside the capital.

Based on average turnout for the many Moral Mondays in Raleigh, early estimates were set at an realistic-seeming, if optimistic, 2,000 to 2,500 possible attendees. That seemed reasonable.

My radio show set up on location, stage right of the main event. We were set to broadcast the entire protest live, from top to bottom, which was something that no one had done for any Moral Monday rally in Raleigh. And for good measure, my pals Mike and Mario from Asheville Channel dot com were doing a live video-stream as well.

Starting at 3 p.m., I began the broadcast with interviews, added updates as the crowds arrived, then planned to go live with the songs, speeches, and the headliner himself, Reverend Barber.

I spoke with elected officials, as well as people who had been arrested, including an Episcopal priest. And, as the first two hours of the show rolled along, people began to arrive. Then more people. Then even more people.

At one point, I looked over to my left, to the small backstage area. And, there he was: Timmy Moffitt! He had the balls to want to address the crowd; he was determined; he demanded the organizers let him up on the stage to speak! He also, I later was told, wanted to speak in person with Rev. Barber.

I took out my phone quickly, to capture this not-to-be-believed moment on camera. But he was turned away, headed off at the pass, by a collective of sweet little old ladies who had taken to calling themselves the "Green Grannies." Then he tried again, and, as I snapped the photo, Cecil Bothwell and Barry Summers were flanking Timmy and helping usher him back toward the exit steps.

What happened next—which I did not see—was that Timmy was surrounded by a horde of teachers, who began pelting him with questions that he could not answer, though he smugly scoffed at the citizens and their concerns. In that group he was also grabbed for a tough Q&A interview by the local monthly *The Urban News*, which challenged him on a number of less-than-honest answers to their questions. It was all caught on video, thanks to one of the crowd's camera.

It was reported that Timmy fled to his nearby car and was last seen driving the wrong way down a one way street.

Of course, he was clearly the single most hated man in town by this point, so you have to question why he was there at all, other than to disrupt the main event and gather publicity for himself. Unless …

Thus far, the Moral Monday Movement had been a long series of well-managed and peaceful protests. The right wing could not finger them for being a mad mob, or out of control, or angry and chaotic. My guess is that Timmy wanted to elicit a huge amount of boos from the audience, perhaps even get a few water bottles thrown, or some such thing. He knew he was hated, and he could see how large this crowd had become. It would be a crowning victory if he could get them to turn ugly, the way his followers in the Tea Party tend to do. THAT would make the front pages. And the GOP would be able to vilify the Movement, as well as Asheville. A clear double victory.

Happily for the world, Timmy was denied. The MM organizers were smarter than that. (Should we be surprised?)

A little before 5 p.m., I looked out to see a sea of faces, signs and flags. I was stunned. It looked like a lot more than the anticipated 2,500 people had gathered.

The event was electrifying, as people spoke openly about their views, their lives, their struggles, and the damage being done by the legislation coming from the leadership in Raleigh. Local leaders and activists spoke, as well as state figures. And all the while, the massive crowd was showering them with love and positive energy.

I had heard clips of Reverend Barber from his previous speeches, and that he was one of the most inspiring speakers of a generation (at the least), and a man of God, cut from a similar cloth as Martin Luther King Jr. But I was not prepared for just how powerful the reverend was.

His speech started low and slow. Very affable. He was a gentle giant, a teddy bear of a man, and though he walked with some discomfort, needing help much of the time, he stood tall; taller than just about any man I had ever been that close to.

Then it started. The low, slow rumble of his voice, as the speech picked up steam, and steadily began to taxi along the runaway of this Asheville crowd, until—suddenly—he achieved a startling liftoff that sent the entire crowd soaring with him to new heights of joy, friendship, camaraderie, and compassion.

It brought tears to eyes, coupled with a chorus of joyous chants and affection from everyone there.

As it ended, I leapt from the stage, and began to make my way through the massive crowd. I had seen it all from a unique perspective, looking out into the crowd. Now I wanted to take a look from their viewpoint.

I began to notice that the crowd extended much further than I could tell from the stage. My god, there were a LOT more than 2,500 people here. Pack Square Park was full, the grassy area beyond the park was full, and the next two blocks, all the way back to the center of town, was full. The crowds spilled out along the sidewalks up and down both sides of the park, and stretched well back beyond the stage, and out of sight.

In my wandering the crowd, as it departed, I ran across local journalists David Forbes and Jake Frankel and we spoke about the event. They confirmed to me that, according to the estimates they were hearing, the crowd was at least between 8,000 and 10,000 people.

This was huge.

The skies had been clear and blue all afternoon, but as the last of the crowd was dispersing, and a couple of lone musicians played on the stage, a few raindrops fell. Within a few minutes, it was a downpour. But the weather had held through the event. And, as if answering the requests of the assembled, the rains fell in a symbolic cleansing.

I retreated to my car, in a nearby parking garage, and called up *The Norman Goldman Show*. They had been awaiting my report once the event had ended. And there, sitting in my car, listening to the rain fall all around, I shared my thoughts with a national audience.

I was changed that day. I had never seen nor experienced such a soul-stirring event. It was powerful. It was something that could be a major game changer. And it could scare the hell out of whoever stands against it. Or tries to.

WORTHY QUOTE:

"The day is over for quick political platitudes. The day is over for little campaign slogans. We've got to build a movement. We've got to think deeper. It's going to take more than a few texts, and a few emails. We must engage in action that shifts the center of political gravity in this nation. And we've got to do it state by state. And we've got to say no matter who's in Congress or who's in the general assemblies of our state or who's in the governor's mansion, or who's in the White House, we've got to demand higher ground. And we've got to say you don't have enough political power to vote us away, you don't have enough insults to talk us away, and you Koch brothers don't have enough damn money to buy us away."

—Reverend William Barber II

Messerism #48

A lot of right-wing folks claim to be followers of Christ. Really. Reality: One, they couldn't pick Christ out of a line-up. Two, the more accurate word for it is "stalkers."

Messerism #73

It's just lucky for the GOP that we aren't a Christian nation, like they said they wanted. I mean, if we were, none of their policies would be allowed. And a lot of them would be stoned. No, not THAT kind of stoned, either.

FOURTEEN
How to Poison a Neighborhood (or Two) and Get Away with It in 10 Easy Steps

In June of 2014, the U.S. Supreme Court ruled against the people in South Asheville's Southside Village, and in favor of the giant electronics company, CTS. If nothing else, they proved that profits are more important than people, and even though—thanks to the same Supreme Court—"corporations are people, my friends," the sum of the parts of the CTS corporation were deemed more valuable than the lives of people who had been poisoned by the company's negligence.

How could SCOTUS rule this way, you may wonder?

Well, thanks to laws in NC, there's a ten-year "period of repose" during which, if no one files a complaint after the company that spilled the chemicals has departed, it's too late: the company gets away with it. So keep the pollution hidden (and the polluting covered up) for ten years and one second, and you can beat the clock, beat the beaten-down people, and get away with it.

But we need to go back to the beginning.

In 1986, CTS closed up shop in Asheville. They departed fully in 1987, leaving behind some sloppy soup of nasty chemicals that had seeped into the ground and begun to migrate. The worst of these is the toxic solvent and cleaning agent Trichloroethylene (TCE), which was banned in most of Europe since the 1970s and has been classified as a human carcinogen and a non-carcinogenic health hazard since 2004 in the U.S.

In the early 1990s Southside Village was built upon some land near the former CTS site, and in 1999 some folks started to put two and two together: they started to realized that, just maybe, some of the cancers, tumors, and chronic illnesses that were working their way through the community might have an identifiable culprit.

In 2002, the Environmental Protection Agency got involved and determined that the situation was dire enough to prompt immediate action. But instead of taking any action, immediate or otherwise, the agency mostly avoided, obfuscated, and ignored the community until 2014, when the date with the Supreme Court seemed to scare the EPA enough to want to at least look busy again, at the site.

Finally, on the Friday before the Monday of the ruling by SCOTUS, the EPA announced that it had evacuated thirteen people, because traces of the highly toxic chemical had turned up in the air tests. But by then the justices had already made their decision.

Tate MacQueen (whom you met in Chapter 11) and his family live in Southside Village, and they're friends and neighbors with many of those affected, as well as having been exposed themselves. As the facts of the long-lasting (and still-ongoing) pollution became apparent, MacQueen became a driving force in trying to uncover the truth of what was going on, and to get solutions. He met with constant resistance, most often from the folks at the EPA, but sometimes even from people in and around the community.

MacQueen had found many allies and a kinship with Jerry Ensminger and folks at Camp Lejeune, where a similar set of circumstances has occurred. In this case, on a U.S. Military base, where, over the time since the chemical spill, around a million men, women, and children had passed through and been exposed, and in some cases died.

I first met MacQueen as a guest on my radio show. I had heard precious little of the CTS site and the swirling scandal that had gone woefully under-reported for years that had turned into decades. He showed me a massive binder containing all the EPA documents along with lots of additional information that he and others had compiled in their pursuit of truth, justice, and the American way. It was an imposing collection—as were the facts contained within. And it was the tip of a much, much bigger iceberg.

Local ABC television channel WLOS TV-13 had hired a new reporter in early 2013. His name was Mike Mason, and he got his hands on the story of CTS. At first skeptical, Mason did his due diligence and submitted a request to the EPA for their documentation on the story.

And, believe it or not, they sent it to him: more than 63,000 pages contained on several DVDs. This documentation made MacQueen's massive binder—more than 500 pages of all of the "known" documents—look pitiful by comparison.

Now no one could doubt that the EPA had been holding out on the community with its full findings. Also included was a path of clarifying clues that revealed gross criminal negligence on the part of the Region 4 EPA folks tasked with handling the CTS site and the community.

Nobody should have been surprised that, within days of sending the DVDs to Mason, the folks at the EPA contacted him again, requesting that he send it all back and destroy any and all copies he may have made, as they did not intend for ALL of that information to get to him. But since they'd released the material to him, they had no legal standing to ask for it back, and Mason moved forward with his investigation ...

... which uncovered a massive CYA (Cover Your Ass) program by the EPA, which led him to filming a documentary report called "Buried Secrets."

A year after the EPA mistakenly sent those 63,000 pages to Mason, the case went before the U.S. Supreme Court. And in spite of the mounting evidence of not just malfeasance by the agency but also a coverup, SCOTUS saw fit to provide CTS with a free pass.

Of course the ruling was a disappointment, but MacQueen and others also saw it as an opportunity to finally get satisfaction from the people who had compounded the initial wrong many times over: the Region 4 EPA officials.

Smelling their own blood in the water after the SCOTUS ruling, many NC GOP politicians, including Timmy Moffitt, began moving to change the laws that had allowed the SCOTUS ruling, which had been greeted with near-universal disapproval by both the CTS and the Camp Lejeune victims. You gotta love election-year politics, when some folks—so many of them Republicans—find their missing moral compasses. Of course, they will lose them again, once re-elected.

That's why, for example, in the run-up to the SCOTUS ruling, Mark Meadows, at a hearing in the spring of 2014, cited the horrors of the CTS contamination site in Asheville, and gave a massive, grandstanding tongue-lashing to an EPA official (see p. 73), which made Meadows look tough but, as usual with Mr. Meadows, led to nothing.

The EPA continued looking busy, and acting like they were super-duper proactive at the CTS site. But it was the efforts of folks like MacQueen that led to the city water lines being extended to the neighborhoods and families at Southside Village.

Mind you, EPA had known, and declared the site as a serious emergency, dating back to 2002. A dozen years later, after getting caught hiding the truth, and a day at the Supreme Court, actual efforts to fix things got underway.

But the obfuscation and manipulation continue, and look to have no end in sight.

Messerism #41

If you're not wealthy, or you're a woman, or a minority, and you're voting for the GOP because of their stance on guns, gays, or abortion, then you're a fool who is voting against your own best interests.

TIGHT-FITTING NATIONAL BRIEFS #2
Stand Your Ground, Shoot to Kill

Summer 2013 brought the not-guilty verdict against paranoid, gung-ho, law-breaking, racially dubious, self-anointed neighborhod watchman George Zimmerman—the man who stalked and chased down the 16-year-old Trayvon Martin and then shot him. At the time he was deliberately disobeying police instructions not to follow the teenage boy but instead to return to his own apartment. But Zimmerman, a former neighborhood watch member who had been rejected by the police when he sought a job, claimed he felt "threatened" by the slightly built Martin, who was wearing a hooded sweatshirt and talking to his girlfriend on his cell phone after going to the nearby store for some Skittles. When Zimmerman went after him, naturally Mr. Martin defended himself against his larger, heavier, stronger, and unidentified armed assailant. He stood his ground. But George Zimmerman had a gun, and Trayvon Martin ended up dead.

The state's "Stand your ground" laws were questionable at best, and foul at worst. And Zimmerman hid behind the laws that Martin had tried to use to defend himself against this bully with a bullet.

Zimmerman walked free.

~~Texas~~. Whoops. Florida.

Of course, trouble followed the trouble-maker, as he ended up being stopped numerous times by law enforcement for traffic violations and the like. He also found himself at the center of a domestic violence issue, when his girlfriend recorded him attacking her; then he called 911 to report it and whined about how poor little George would be misunderstood and misrepresented in the media.

I understand quite well. George is a thug, a poor example of a human being, and he got away with ... what most people would call murder.

And he went free.

Oh, and lest we forget the massive fraud he and his then-wife committed by raising funds off the easily-duped right wing-iverse that automatically supported him because ... gun rights, and because ... self-pitying white victim, and because ... dangerous black teen thug (obviously up to no good, and guilty of something, because they all are).... At any rate, he failed to report those funds when he went looking for handouts in the way of legal support to get him off the hook.

So maybe after we kick Texas out of the Union (see Messerism #23, p. 102), we should Bugs Bunny Florida by hack-sawing it off and pushing it out to sea.

War crimes? He said, she said

Around the same time that Zimmerman was walking tall and free, Private Bradley Manning was sent up for having exposed war-crime-type activity, while he was in the Army serving in the George W. Bush wars of idiocy of the 2000s.

Of course, Manning, as a soldier, had signed away some of the rights he was fighting to protect for the rest of us. So his moral outrage at the war crimes was actually not something he had any right to reveal. A technicality, I know, but a fact.

To top it all off, amid the whole thing, Manning came out of the closet, declaring that he was actually a she in male casings, and was beginning to change his life to a her life, and now preferred to be called Chelsea Manning.

Nothing wrong there. The timing, of course, probably didn't help the case in the court of public opinion. Especially for the right wing who just can't process such concepts without their heads popping like Belloque at the end of *Raiders of the Lost Ark*. So Manning, unlike Zimmerman, is serving a prison sentence.

FIFTEEN
ZEN AND THE ART OF VAGINA MAINTENANCE

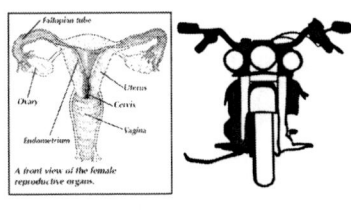

Vague resemblance: the human female (l); a motorcycle (r)

What does the female reproductive system have to do with motorcycles?

Other than a vague resemblance (and Republicans thinking they're both unsafe), not a lot. Unless you're in North Carolina, and passing radical right-wing legislation with the skill and finesse of an epileptic brain surgeon using a chainsaw instead a scalpel and undergoing a seizure while operating.

Part of the radical-right agenda that took power in NC was an old, hackneyed hate of *Roe v. Wade*—which happened over four decades ago. (Can we say, "Get over it!"?)

Southern states are always looking for ways to screw women—especially to keep them from making their own choices about their bodies. I'm sure that the attitude in the GOP about the 1950s being "the good old days" has a lot to do with the fact that minorities were supposed to stay at their own "colored" water fountains, and not sit at the lunch counter, and ride in the back of the bus—and good little white women got married straight out of high school, cooked real well, and stayed silently barefoot and pregnant.

At least I assume that's why they revere the 1950s so much. I mean, they couldn't love the '50s on account of the tax rate on the wealthiest, which was way more than double what it is now; or the fact that more than a third of all household breadwinners were union men (and some women); or that corporate taxes made up more than 30% of federal revenue, compared to 10% today; or that the socialist Eisenhower administration was building a nationalized system of interstate highways and railing against the military-industrial complex. Remember that era, and those policies that led to one-career households and a middle class that looked like *Leave It To Beaver*?

Anyway, in the infinite unwise wise-guy wisdom of the right wing, our rulers in Raleigh found the most creative of ways to strike against women's clinics across the state. They hid it in a motorcycle safety bill.

Let me repeat: a motorcycle safety bill.

Because of the obvious connection between the two.

Puppet Pat McCrory took some heat for this, since he was on record in his campaign vowing to not sign any measure attempting to restrict access for women. His excuse for this new law? Safety concerns, not restrictions.

Follow that with a surprise inspection to the FemCare clinic in Asheville, and shutting it down after applying new rules (ones that apply to surgical environments within major hospital facilities.) And so, two days after McCrory signed it into law, the Department of Health and Human Services suspended the license for FemCare.

FemCare provided women's health services including annual exams, birth control, and screenings for sexually transmitted diseases.

The State Health Director resigned soon after, citing policy differences with the new administration.

FemCare re-opened and had its license restored by the end of August 2013, after meeting the list of new standards for operation and safety. But the FemCare property was put up for sale in March of 2014.

By July 2014, WNC'S only clinic for abortions closed in Asheville, with plans to build and open a new site. However, there is nothing there to fill the void in the meantime.

TIGHT-FITTING NATIONAL BRIEFS #3
Edward Snowden, to Russia with Love

Secrets-maven Edward Snowden used his position as a contract employee within the National Security Agency to create more than a few ripples in the summer of 2013, when in an interview with British magazine *The Guardian* he revealed a bunch of details about data-gathering.

The most shocking part of the story—about how the NSA has been spying rather widely on just about anyone and everyone—isn't that they've been doing it, but that people were actually surprised.

All you had to do was check out all of the people who checked in on FourSquare, at their local Starbucks, on an un-secure server (they just clicked "OK") to log onto Twitter to protest the loss of their privacy. Or watch what happened in Boston after the April 15 bombing (see p. 43).

Nope. We've been surrendering privacy, hand over Tweet, at a rapid pace for the better part of a decade.

You couldn't legitimately be surprised, but you certainly could be massively pissed off. Simply track backward to the Patriot Act, which was enacted in 2001, supposedly in response to 9/11. You know, 2001!? Before Facebook, YouTube, Twitter, Instagram, FourSquare, and smartphones with that handy skill of locating you if you log in. Hell, it was written before there was MySpace!

There was no way that anyone could have planned for technology to advance so rapidly. And the outdated Patriot Act has plenty of loose loopholes that folks like the NSA easily slipped through.

What was stunning was the fact that Snowden, with his smug air of self-importance in his act of patriotic defiance, found himself on the run, thinking he was a modern-day whistle-blowing 007 super-agent for the public. Instead, thanks to those good ol' PATRIOT ACTions, there was nothing about what he exposed that was actually illegal! All the wiretapping, information-gathering, snooping, and spying was permitted. In fact, it turned out that Snowden himself was the only one who actually committed a crime.

Doesn't matter whether you like him, support him, or agree with him, that's the way it shakes out.

Ironic that the only place he could find asylum was that bastion of civil liberties, Russia, which took him in for a year. That year expired in late July of 2014, but at the end of the summer Czar Vladimir Putin granted him an extra three years of asylum, and this fall Snowden has been announcing that he plans to learn the language. Of course, after another three years most of America won't even remember who he is. Thank you, short attention span!

Maybe his next move should be getting a striped shirt, a hat and scarf, and just disappear into a large crowd somewhere. I mean, he does sort of look like the kid from *Where's Waldo*.

Messerism #77

We've ended up with a two-party system in this country, where there's very little difference between them. It's a lot like living with two drunken, abusive parents. The only difference is that one of them at least feels bad about beating the crap out of you afterward.

SIXTEEN
WEST CAROLINA, AN OLD NEW IDEA. OR, HOW TO MAKE A STATE AND A STATEMENT

The last time a state was formed by breaking away from another state was 1863, when West Virginia left the old Commonwealth over slavery and Civil War disagreements. And certainly that was a justifiable thing to do, given the day and age and issues surrounding them both. It probably helped that there was a war on, and the U.S. Congress happily endorsed the move.

You have to wonder about statehood, and why there hasn't been something like that since then.

Sure, political calculations and red tape certainly may have played a role. And a lot of people would probably be shocked to learn that the talk of new statehood is hardly a new concept.

In June of 2013, I caught myself with a spare five minutes of radio air time that I had not bothered to plan for. A small oversight. So, during the commercial break, I scoured the Internet looking for a short, fun story to share. And, lo and behold, I hit upon the hot talk of North Colorado.

It seems a bunch of folks in Colorado were up in arms over the state's moves to clean up the environment and better manage guns. Apparently the new Democratic governor and legislature were just a tad too liberal for the Centennial State. Typical right-winger joke, right? Boo-hoo, the whiners protest clean air and gun safety, and decide to secede.

So, I ran with it. And half way through it, I joked that, based on these complaints, maybe more states should have this happen. Then, the lightbulb moment hit me: the North Carolina state GOP was trying to take away the Asheville water system, and privatize it, so why should we not do the same thing here?

If Asheville loses the lawsuit to keep its water, then we should just declare statehood, call it West Carolina, and have our own do-over. After all, the mountains of WNC are nothing like the rest of the state, either socially or geographically. And, for as long as I can remember, there's been a WNC mantra about the state government thinking that the state ended where the mountains began; we've always felt like the redheaded stepchild in this state (no offense intended to adopted gingers who may be reading this.)

In the days and weeks that followed, I suddenly became aware of the whole statehood movement out there in the nation, and learned about a variety of different attempts at statehood, both throughout our history and, today, all across the country.

There have been well over one hundred attempts at statehood since our nation's formation, including a major one in our own back yard in the form of the state of Franklin, to be named for Ben Franklin (an attempt to get his endorsement, which they did not), and consisting of what is currently Eastern Tennessee. That had previously been part of North Carolina, which originally went all the way to the Mississippi River, and that part was sold off as a way of paying off Revolutionary War debt. It turns out Raleigh's dismissive attitude toward the mountain region started waaaaaay back.

More recently, there are people pushing to break California into multiple states, one of which would be called "Jefferson." (Seeing a trend? Hope they realize that he's dead and can't grant his approval.) There's also "Superior," which would comprise the Northern end of Michigan. Even little Maryland even wants to break into two. And, lest we forget, Washington, DC, which is the nation's capital, as well as the only place in the country that has the one thing that led most to the Revolutionary War: taxation without representation.

So, there are quite a few places out there looking to start over, with a new state.

What happened after I filled that five minutes of air time, was both impressive and surprising. The sentiment caught hold. In a big, big way.

One of the executives at the radio station came into my studio a few days later and asked me what I had been talking about it on air. I was a bit cautious, not sure where that conversation was headed. Perhaps he sensed my trepidation, and immediately said, "The numbers are way up, so whatever you're doing, keep it up!"

Suddenly, people were calling in, passionately wanting to talk about the concept.

There were some who pointed me toward a number of folks who had been having similar conversations, bubbling under about a decade earlier. I had not heard of it then, and the whole idea that I put out there came out quite randomly. But I embraced the idea that others had thought of it already, and were continuing to endorse the notion.

It became an ongoing pet cause on the show, and the enthusiasm was impressive.

Of course, there were skeptics and detractors.

One of the first points that someone made against it, was that, based on the overall rural, conservative makeup of the region—Asheville being another of Carl Sagan-like Little Blue Dot, only in the redness of the state and not the blackness of space—and on the political tiger pit of modern partisanship brainwashing, West Carolina would instantly become a shiny new RED state, giving the Senate two more right-wingers, as well as one or two more righties in the House.

It was a quandary, no doubt.

My reply?

If we're starting fresh, why would we even want to play by the old house rules? Right? New state, new set of rules.

If we have a clean slate, who's to say that we can't make it part of our new foundation that our new (and improved) state would be a non-partisan state? Find a way to get money out of politics, and don't allow candidates to declare party affiliation. Everyone has to run as independents, who, once they win, can caucus however they choose (and suffer at the hands of the voters back home, if they chose poorly.)

We're all tricked into thinking that we have to stick by the old rules and regulations that are clearly no longer working effectively for anyone except the people getting elected to power, then running amok.

We have to stop filtering our thoughts, our principles, our morals, and our humanity through the cracked prisms of the Democratic and Republican party standards. Both parties benefit from keeping the population divided, and fighting over minutiae, while they ransack from within, claiming the support and mandates of the results of low-turnout elections.

If only we can talk to one another without putting a parenthetical "D" or "R" out front. Once you claim one of those two letters, you taint the conversation, as the person you are trying to talk to about real issues can't help but assign political party stereotypes. It hurts the honesty of the conversation, and it needs to be done away with.

In doing so, we will discover that we all have more in common than we've been led to believe. And it will fundamentally change the way we view the polluted partisanship of politics.

How would something so radical work, you may ask?

Think of small states. Vermont, Rhode Island. Ever hear about the same level of chaos and turmoil coming from them that you hear about in places like Florida, California, Texas, and any other large state with a large population. Montana and Alaska are too sparsely populated for anyone to get into too much trouble. Especially now that Alaska got abandoned by Sarah Palin, who went away to plague the Lower 48.

I've concluded that smaller is better.

In state size. Just state size. (Don't go there.)

It would be easier to manage a smaller state. It would be easier to shut out the big money of partisan politics, and it would take the focus back to a more local level. You can't tell me there's something bad in that idea!

Think of it: West Carolina could become a beacon of hope for other states looking to fix the ills and ugliness of what politics has become.

We could become a state that bans Monsanto crops, and revert to the almost lost agrarian practices of generations past, and become the nation's leading state of non-GMO based crops.

We could build giant wind farms, and solar panel fields, and become more energy efficient. Additionally, our geographic advantage of bordering five other states (South Carolina, what's left of North Carolina, Georgia, Tennessee and Virginia) could mean that we could cross those borders and provide clean energy alternatives to our neighbors.

By sending non-partisan delegates to Washington, DC, to represent us, we could shame those there who thrive on the gridlock, and create the inefficient and ineffective process we now endure. And, in shaming the Democrats and Republicans, we could inspire other states to move in our direction, and perhaps embolden Independent candidates and inspire a Three-, Four-, even Five-Party mentality.

Unlike North Colorado, our intent would not be a tantrum to shun the state government, and be contrarians. No. We could use this as a platform of reform and resuscitation of true Democracy.

It isn't impossible. Sure, it will be a lot of long, hard work. But it would be worth it. And we could be stronger as a result.

It could be the very change that this floundering nation needs.

Before it's too late.

Some will scoff, and call it a pipe dream. But this country was founded by those who were brave enough to ignore the detractors and skeptics.

West Carolina could be the most patriotic thing to happen to this country in a very long time.

And—the best bonus of all—its capital would be Asheville, Beer City, USA!

Messerism #86

Is it just me, or does Cuban Canadian Texas Senator Ted Cruz look like a badly drawn Doonesbury character that Gary Trudeau rejected?

Speaking of Texas:
If Texas were to go away, or go blue, Electoral-College math would make it mathematically impossible for the GOP to win the White House ever again. And it's already starting to turn a nice shade of purple.

And speaking of Ted Cruz:
Messerism #39

Red is a color of danger and warning. Red Scare! Red Sky at dawning, sailors take warning! Code Red! Red State! Is it any wonder that the GOP chose RED? And how is it no one sees the irony?

That's what I call "The Messerism Triple Threat." Or "Triple Treat."

TIGHT-FITTING NATIONAL BRIEFS #4
Grand Rand Takes a Stand, or, Drone Wars, Episode I

Between the NSA spying, as revealed by Edward Snowden, and the record number of drone strikes against the "enemy" abroad by the president, more than a few true-blue liberals were less than happy with the man they (twice) helped put into the White House.

And in a moment of nonpartisanship, they found a strange bedfellow in the Jheri-curled Tea-Party wonder from Kentucky that is Rand Paul: Rand, Son of Ron, the Libertarian GOP darling of the folks who want it all, but don't want any responsibility.

I once heard that Libertarians are like cats: they think they are independent and act like they could care less about their human companions. Until it's feeding time or the litter box is full, then they need the shit out of you.

Well, in summer of 2013, Rand decided the time was right to gRand-stand and make some speeches to crowds of young people who were suddenly hearing the horror stories of the NSA and the White House having access to their private emails, texts, sexts, and whatnots on their smartphones.

Rand gained a lot of traction with that young and restless crowd. This gave establishment Democrats some serious pause, as they were counting on those same young, dumb, and full of cum kids to be wildly liberal. Too bad the Democratic Party isn't even liberal on a tame level these days.

It was a stunning turn of events, as a large number of the doveish folks on the left found great appeal in what Rand had to say. I even had to agree with him on some of those points.

No doubt, Hillary Clinton did more double takes than she did when Bill used to come home late smelling of cheap wine, perfume, and lady bits.

And, no one was more crestfallen than Ted Cruz, who was the Tea Party hopeful for one of the top crazy slots in 2016. Suddenly Rand was the darling, and Teddy found himself demoted to the category of Batshit, second class.

Messerism #66

I once approached a street-preacher type who was condemning everyone he saw as they passed by during a huge festival in downtown Asheville. I stopped and asked how it was exactly that he knew that everyone else around, but him, was damned. He had no answer. Then I asked him who he voted for in the last election (2004). He hemmed and hawed a bit, until finally he sheepishly said, George W. Bush. Then I asked him if he had given any thought to the scripture that warns of false prophets, and whether or not he had perhaps fallen victim of the very thing his good book warns against? Again, he had no answer. And he was silent for a good long while, as I walked away.

REAL LIFE INTERRUPTION #4

Amid all the politics and protests, other aspects of life continued apace, as well.

I had a play of mine set to world-premiere in late September, which was taking a good deal of time and attention. I was spending most evenings at Parkway Playhouse.

Parkway is one of the state's oldest professional theatres, and I had been working with them regularly since 2004. They have a first-look option (unofficially) for most of the new material I write, and the Producing Artistic Director, Andrew Gall, is one my nearest and dearest friends.

Not to say that I didn't have some free time. I did. And, with it, I spent much of it going to live concerts with Kelli. We even took her kids and mine to Carowinds Amusement Park in Charlotte, and to a Train concert, in late July.

In August, Kelli and I saw a number of great shows: *Under the Summer Sun with Gin Blossoms, Sugar Ray, Vertical Horizon, Fastball and Smash Mouth*, *Onerepublic* with Mayer Hawthorne, and finally, the 30th Anniversary "Sports" album tour by Huey Lewis and The News.

My first music love as a teen was Huey and the News, so this was already a special show for me. But I had something a little more up my sleeve.

I had booked us a hotel just around the corner from the venue in Knoxville. The band was notorious throughout their career for always coming back to their hotel bar and hanging out after shows. You just had to know where they were staying.

I was gambling that this was the place, and as we entered the lobby, I saw the band's tour manager standing there, looking at his watch.

We checked in, and I told Kelli that this was where the band were staying. Then, as we went to the elevator, the doors opened, and Huey

Lewis himself stepped right out in front of me. He was talking on his cell phone, but he saw my concert T-Shirt, and gave me a quick, affirming look, a nod, and a distinct "Hey!"

I was dumbfounded. Kelli was quite surprised too. Timing is everything.

The show was great, and afterward we rushed back and staked ourselves out in the lobby, waiting for the band to return. After a while they did, coming from behind us, from an entrance closer to the hotel bar.

We quickly went to the bar, and saw Huey and several other band members already there.

We made friends with a man named Ken, who had seen us at the show, and we all three hung out for a good long while, wondering when and how to approach THEM. Finally, Ken asked the waitress to buy Huey and his lady friend a drink.

Drinks were delivered, and we got a nice look and wave.

Huey's lady friend came over to thank us, and we waited for a while longer before approaching. When we did, Huey could not have been nicer and more gracious. He signed my tour poster, posed for a couple of photos, and chatted us up a bit.

We went back to our table. I was floating. I'd met one of my childhood heroes! But, now that I had a tiny taste, I wanted some more.

The other guys in the band were all there by now, and I took a page from Ken's book and send a drink over to Johnny Colla, one of the main songwriters as well as sax player. He had always been one of my favorite guys in the band.

Fast forward: Johnny came over to chat, signed the poster, and took some pictures as well. And finally, drummer Bill Gibson passed by, and I stopped him. We chatted a good bit, since he is the one band member to spend a good amount of time on the Band's website forum.

It was a Monday night in August, in Knoxville, and we stayed until the bitter end, shutting down the bar with Huey Lewis and The News.

Next day, I was back at the regular radio gig, thinking that it couldn't get much better than last night, when my Program Director, Brian Hall, stopped me and said that he had spoken to John Fugelsang, who was in town visiting family, and wandered if we would mind him stopping by the show and chatting.

John Fugelsang! Comedian extraordinaire! The guy who, a year before, while a guest on the CNN morning show *Starting Point*, got one of Mitt Romney's main spokespeople to use the now-infamous Etch-a-sketch comment!

John Fugelsang: "Is there a concern that the pressure from Santorum and Gingrich might force the governor to tack so far to the right that it might hurt him with moderate voters in the general election?"

Eric Fehnstrom: "Well, I think you hit a reset button for the fall campaign. Everything changes. It's almost like an Etch-a-sketch—you can kind of shake it up, and we start all over again."

John not only spoiled Romney's week (and perhaps election), but he helped sell more Etch-a-sketches than any time since the 1970s. And he wanted to know if it was all right if he stopped by?

He stayed on air with me for the last 90 minutes of my show, taking calls, cracking jokes, and having an all-around good time.

As I walked him out, I told him that he was welcome back anytime he was in town. He had mentioned that he had a flight the next day at 6 p.m., and I jokingly offered to have him back the next show, until he had to leave.

To my surprise, he said he would love to. Then he asked if I was sure, and insisted that he didn't want to impose. Seriously! The guy could not have been a nicer, humbler guy.

So, the next day, John was back at 3, and we had another fun hour and a half of radio.

To this day, when we take a day off, one of my producers—Jim Meyer—will program one or those two Fugelsang episodes to replay as a "Best of" show.

I was on a run of great days that last week of August, 2013!

My play, *Sherlock Holmes Returns*, opened on September 20, but it was the week before that delivered the biggest moment of being brought back to earth.

As rehearsal drew to a close on Thursday evening, September 12, I got a frantic call from my mother. My uncle Ray, her younger brother, had been taken to the hospital after collapsing while mowing the lawn.

Ray and his family lived in upstate South Carolina, and my mother was rushing there. A few hours later she called with the news of his passing.

It hit me like the proverbial ton of bricks, and so, as I processed it, I did what comes naturally, and I wrote about it:

> September 12, 2013:
> I just learned of the passing of my uncle. I had gotten word that he was taken to the hospital a few hours ago, and it was not good. Confirmation just came. It struck me that I was at a rehearsal for the upcoming world premiere of my new script, and I got word while there tonight working on the show, and how my desire to become a writer, a storyteller, an entertainer was born on a late summer night when I was 7, and my fun uncle, Ray, took me and my cousin Mike Russell, to the drive-in movie theatre in Waynesville, to see *Star Wars*. He was the cool, fun uncle, and he knew that he wanted his two nephews to see this incredible movie. It really changed my life. It helped shape me, in who I would aspire to be and become. He taught us to play Monopoly one night over some frosty mugs of root beer and pepperoni pizza from Pizza Hut (this was a BIG deal in the late 1970s). And he bought us a set of young classic novels one Christmas, among which was a copy of *Robin Hood*. Needless to say, I owe him a great debt for being there and being willing to let a couple of young boys tag along. He was only 59 years old, as of just a few weeks ago. Too young. Too good. There are too few good ones left out there, and we lost a great one today.

I spoke at his funeral, recounting much of what I had written those few days earlier. And Mike and I were together throughout the funeral, sharing the memories of those bonds of our childhood because of this great, loving man, who took two goofy young boys under his wing and made us feel special.

We got a bit turned around on the way to the cemetery, and ended up being the last to arrive. As I got out of the car, and looked up ahead at the gathered pockets of family and friends in one grouping, and for a fleeting moment, as I was looking away, I could have sworn that I saw my uncle. Not as he was, but a good deal younger, and wearing a bright blue shirt among the seas of gray and black.

When I looked back, he was gone.

Perhaps my eyes were playing tricks.

Perhaps not.

And, within the hour, one of my other childhood heroes—but not one from afar—was laid to rest. And a part of who I was and who I had become because of him, in that moment, began to burn hotter and brighter.

In his memory, I vowed to keep writing, keep creating, keep bettering myself, and never lose hope or belief in what I can accomplish.

Sherlock Holmes Returns was a success, and the published editions arrived a few days later. Each moment of each night of the performance, Uncle Ray was in my thoughts. Oddly enough—or ironically, or presciently—that collection of classics that he had given me on that long-ago Christmas also contained the Sherlock Holmes mystery *The Hound of the Baskervilles*.

Messerism #55

Since Conservatives made "Liberal" a dirty word back in the days of Reagan, perhaps it is past time for the modern Progressives to rebrand the right wing, as "Regressives." It does accurately describe the modern GOP and the direction they are trying to take America.

SEVENTEEN
OBAMACARE SCORN, AND I DON'T CARE! MY MASTER'S GONE AWAY!

Ah, Mark Meadows. He's one of ours. We have to take the blame for his dubious actions in our names on the floor of the U.S. House of Representatives.

But, Ted Cruz? Oh, no. No, no, no. He's not our fault. Blame him on the U.S. Senate! Blame him on Texas. Blame Canada! Blame Cuba! Just don't look at any of us in NC. We can cook up crazy, but nothing along the size of the giant bats that swirl in that lunatic, McCarthy-lite belfry.

Unlike chocolate and peanut butter, when you mix Meadows and Cruz, it is not a great taste. And it can get costly.

The U.S. Supreme Court has developed a strong sense of schizophrenia in recent years. It was baffling to see the decidedly right-leaning Court rule (randomly at times, it seemed) in favor of more progressive notions. This sends the GOP right round the bend—like when they overturned the Defense of Marriage Act, allowing same sex marriage a clear path in this nation. But no ruling irked the right more than when SCOTUS gave a full-on, green-lights-all-the-way-home to the Affordable Care Act, better known as ObamaCare.

Yessiree, it was a done deal, thanks to a classification with the nation's tax laws.

And, come October 1, 2013, it was open for business and would be well on its way to becoming as common as Medicare, Social Security, and any other of those lefty, pinko, commie things that every old conservative now fights tooth and nail to hang onto.

But first, let's go back a few steps in this story.

ObamaCare was not very popular. No mistake about that. And a lot of cable news talking heads happily shouted out, and jumped up and down about the clear plurality of people who were "opposed" to the new law.

What the chatterers failed to point out—time and time again—was the fact that, among those "opposed" people, about half were from the progressive left who didn't think the law went far enough.

Of course, they would be correct. And they had reason to be wary. After all, ObamaCare was nothing more than a retread of RomneyCare in Massachusetts, which itself was an almost exact copy of the health care alternatives proposed in the early 1990s as a right-wing alternative to then-First-Lady Hillary Clinton's health initiative (remember "Hillarycare"?). Bob Dole's 1996 campaign supported the same basic plan, and why not? It was developed by the right-wing, ultra-conservative, big-business-supported Heritage Foundation as a way to force citizens to buy private health insurance from their huge, for-profit companies. A perfect GOP program of corporate welfare!

So, basically, Obama ended up going with a long-rejected GOP-endorsed plan. And the modern GOP immediately pulled a 180 Uey into 101% opposition to their own plans (exactly the way John McCain had done on the campaign trail to his own immigration legislation).

But, in this day and age of highly-charged, highly-illogical partisan politics, a half-bad, business friendly old GOP plan seems downright plausible to people who are struggling, and have no health care coverage, and cannot afford insurance.

Despite their opposition, the law passed, was signed, and (except for the required growth in Medicaid enrolment) withstood a Supreme Court challenge—and it immediately faced some of the most ridiculous political nonsense that I've heard in my lifetime.

The frothing far right were positively apoplectic at the thought of being forced to get healthy. And they were worked into a further froth by Texas Senator Ted Cruz, whose arrogance far overshadowed his common sense.

Ted is all about chest-thumping and bomb-throwing as his form of political service. And he found a willing accomplice in NC's 11th District Congressional Representative, Mark Meadows, who went above and beyond to push for a full government shutdown.

Meadows, elected in 2012, wrote a letter that suggested to party leaders that they could kill Obamacare by enacting a complete shutdown of the government. The logic was that by cutting off all funds to run the government, the White House and Democrats would be so desperate to get tax money rolling in again that they'd sacrifice Obamacare if the entire GOP held firm. And in August of 2013, eight months after the freshman Republican had sworn his oath to "faithfully discharge the duties of the office on which I am about to enter," he managed to get about eighty Republicans to sign onto his letter to House Speaker John Boehner.

Now, one of those "duties of the office" is to write a budget, but that's almost irrelevant, because what Mark's grand scheme missed was any realization that a government shutdown would not de-fund Obamacare. Its funding is separate from the operating budget. (One can ponder how it is that so many members of Congress could not have known that, but it might give you a mild stroke.)

But reality could not deter this band of idiots. So, as of October 1, 2013, the government was shut down. And, at that exact same moment, as the clock ticked over to 12:00:01 a.m., Obamacare became the full-fledged law of the land! Folks could start to register for and purchase insurance plans immediately.

Well ... maybe not so immediately, as the grand genius of the people setting up the program, massively, in the word of George Dubya Bush, "misunderestimated" the desire of people to get insured. The website was a mess, it crashed, it was slow, it was inefficient, and people were getting frustrated with it.

Of course, the GOP pointed to the website overload as proof of failure and incompetence by the president. (Apparently, in their wee little brains, Mr. Obama himself was the website designer.) Never mind that the reason for the website problems could be attributed to—at least in part—extreme interest on the part of the public. Also, it could be blamed on stubborn GOP states that refused to set up in-state exchanges for people to register with, forcing the federal government to try to build a site that created a separate exchange for each of the thirty-three states that had refused to create their own.

Thanks to states, including North Carolina, that forced their citizens to rely on the federal website, the number of people trying to access Healthcare.gov was much larger than the site was designed to handle.

Maybe that was part of the plan. After all, a crashed website demonstrates the demand. At least, that's what I would have led with. However, as usual, the Obama administration seemed to not want to brag, but instead let the GOP beat them up over the failings of the website—which was a thing the GOP actually didn't want to work in the first place! Oh, the irony.

And, at the same time, the government was closed for business—thanks to Mark Meadows pushing his agenda.

Of course, October 1 was a bad time for such a thing, especially in the 11th District, which includes a massive portion of the Blue Ridge Parkway, and where a vast proportion of the economy is based on tourism. October is the area's most popular month, as millions of people converge on the mountains to see the fall colors. Many, or even most, of them drive along the Parkway—which, under Meadowsgate, was closed and padlocked.

By the time the Meadows shutdown actually happened, however, the congressman was in the background of this tale, as Ted Cruz—from the Senate—had pushed House Speaker Boehner out of his way to lead the House's anarchy. The Cuban-Canadian Texasshole was the loudest and proudest, most chaotic merrymaker in all of DC.

But Meadows deserves a lot of the credit for this folly. His district, and those surrounding it in NC and Tennessee, suffered a conservative estimate of $1,000,000 per day in economic losses due to the shutdown.

His name appeared—with the blame—in *The Washington Post*, and *The New Yorker*, and the local *Citizen-Times*, and by the time the roars of outrage were being heard, he was nowhere to be found, or heard. He was quite happy to be a partner in the Cruz demolition machine, a silent partner other than claiming that he had had nothing to do with it. Meadows was harder to find in those days of economic crumble for his home district than a member of the KKK at a Wu Tang Clan reunion tour. I'm almost surprised that he didn't try to convince people he'd voted against the shutdown.

Mark Meadows represents someone. But it's clearly not anyone in his district.

In spite of all the problems around the Obamacare launch, and despite McCrory and Tillis and Moffitt's herculean efforts to block it, the good ol' Tarheel State quickly became fifth nationwide in overall enrollment, following Florida, Texas, New York, and California. Impressive.

And, as the world knows, the website bugs were fixed fairly soon, and eventually more and more people were able to sign up and get themselves insured for perhaps the first time ever.

Even though much of the Affordable Care Act was cribbed from a twenty-year-old GOP platform plank, Repubs were spitting mad that their own mediocre idea, which had never been taken seriously, was now somehow working, and that a Democrat had made it work. And not just any Democrat. Barack Hussein Obama. Kenyan. Fascist. Communist. Muslim. Arab-lover. Community organizer. Hawaiian. Tyrant. Wimp. Golfer. Damn!

Under Obamacare, insurance companies were suddenly held to somewhat stronger standards, after running roughshod over their own customers for decades. No longer could they reject people for previously-existing conditions. Or refuse to pay for coverage people had contracted for. Or stop paying after costs hit a magical (and never-before-disclosed) "maximum payout amount." Or double- and triple-bill the government for basic procedures.

Now they had to spend 80% on actual healthcare, and not on marketing, outlandish CEO pay ($20+million a year, anybody?), and hoity-toity retreats for top executives. Now kids could stay on their parents' plans until age 26. Now anyone could sign up and even get a subsidy. All good things, right?

Of course, the media tried to chum the water by pointing out that a "surprising" number of young people 18-24 were not signing up. "Oh, dear," the media wrung its collective hands, "that could spell doom for the whole thing!!"

Until you go back up a few lines and re-read the part where kids can stay on their parents' plans until age 26.

Well, in spite of the fact that insurance companies were now getting eight million new customers signed up to pay them monthly premiums, which would spell millions and millions in additional profits, the GOP were determined to get rid of this horrible, terrible, bad, horrific, people-killing, job-killing, will-killing, thrill-killing piece of (formerly Republican) legislation—legislation that would certainly spell the irrevocable doom and destruction of Mom, apple pie, and all things sweet and dear in America.

The House of Representatives, led by Speaker John Boehner, voted more than fifty times to repeal it. This failed to go anywhere, however, as it would have to also pass the Senate controlled by Democrats. And if it did that, it would then have to be signed into law by the president. That's right, the success of repeal would depend upon the agreement of the man who'd gotten it enacted into law—part of his party's platform for sixty years, since Harry Truman called for national health insurance. The man who'd done what Harry, and JFK, and LBJ, and even Bill Clinton couldn't get done. (Jimmy Carter didn't really try during his four years in office.)

Fifty times they voted to repeal the ACA ... and we pay them hefty salaries to do this.

I did notice one thing that the majority of people who stood so vocally opposed to Obamacare all seemed to have in common: they're all already insured. Well insured. Many of them with taxpayer-supported Medicare. And Congress, despite voting over and over again against others having insurance, is a prime example of living on a socialized, publicly subsidized insurance program.

The term "hypocrite" certainly is getting a workout these days.

As the one-year anniversary approaches of Obamacare going into full effect (some parts of the law rolled out during the first two years after it was signed into law), projections indicated that somewhere over 10,000,000 people now have coverage that hadn't previously been insured. That's more than 7.5 million with policies they're paying premiums for (either in full or, if they get subsidies, in part), plus several million more individuals, families, and children enrolled in Medicaid in he states that expanded it (unlike, alas, North Carolina). And during the next sign-up period, no doubt millions more will join the ranks of the newly insured.

Of course, not only did North Carolina's regime refuse to establish a state-run exchange for customers, but they also refused the funding of the Medicaid Expansion portions of the Affordable Care Act. Which cost the state $500 billion over the next ten years, and 500,000 people left uncovered, and 50,000 lost jobs ... to say nothing of massive cutbacks at many of the state's hospitals.

And, in at least one case, the eventual shutdown of the privately-run hospital in Belhaven, NC, whose owners said that without the additional funding, they "couldn't afford" to keep it operating. In response, in July of 2014 the Republican Mayor of Belhaven walked the almost 300 miles from his town to Washington, DC. He wanted to protest the funding cuts and to highlight the actual, measurable, human damage that the NC GOP's refusal to cooperate with the law of the land was having on real citizens.

Of course, I should point out that his real beef was with the GOP-run government of North Carolina, and not Washington, DC. But it sure did get more attention. It would have been scuttled in the state press, for sure.

Messerism #56

I remember that old joke about "Pro" being the opposite of "Con." Which makes Congress the opposite of Progress. Sometimes it is really written out for you, in black and white. Not sure why people can't see it.

EIGHTEEN
Everything Else from 2013, in 10 Easy Bullet Points

Before we escape 2013, here are a few highlights that were otherwise missed:
- Holy smoke! We got a new Pope (not Art). And the old one (the one who looked a little like an old Nazi, and a lot like The Emperor from *Star Wars*) was still hanging around, which has never happened before (they're supposed to die, not retire, but he didn't get the memo). The new guy, Pope Francis, turned out to be a pretty radical dude, who actually seemed to be interested in the Christian message of the Bible—you know, feed the hungry, clothe the poor, love your enemy, and all that—and acted accordingly. This, of course, upset the Catholic establishment, along with the GOP. All that "Christ" talk is really bad for business.
- *American Idol's* Clay Aiken decides to run for Congress. Against Renee Ellmers (you already read ALL about her). His nearest competitor, who barely lost the primary to Aiken, died (really).
- Fake reality show *Duck Dynasty* gets in a jam. Not apple, grape, or strawberry. The head (multimillionaire) Duck-head said some wildly homophobic things, followed by a small dumptruckful of racist things. He gets an official slap on the wrist, but gets called out for the ridiculous backwards, backwoods hick he is. Then he gets defended by people who might actually be dumb enough to either support him, or think that what they watch isn't scripted on the "reality" show. Ratings ended up dropping for the Duckers. And real photos surface, showing the younger stars of the show,

as young college preppy pricks, raising questions about whether any of it is actually real, or if the dopes who watch have been duped.

- Keystone XL Pipeline becomes a political circus. The incredibly dirty tar sands oil controversy led some to support it for the jobs it would bring (3,000 temps, less than forty permanent full-time), and some to think that we would somehow benefit from letting the Big Oil folks use the center of the nation as a pipeline to get dirty oil to the Gulf of Mexico, then sell it on the international market. The president actually considered supporting it, and plenty of folks lost their minds. Leading to some pretty serious protests to counter the advanced White House waffling.
- Current Obama-haters hate that he uses weaponized drones. But when the FAA announced plans from web sales giant Amazon to have delivery drones, the appeal of commercial application made many people dream of 30-minutes-or-less delivery of stuff. Just don't go outside during the last couple of days before Christmas, lest you get beaned by a last-minute shopper's drone delivery.
- Billy Graham celebrated his 95th birthday in November. The ailing Preacher's sycophant son, Franklin, threw a right-wing Grove Park Inn bash for the addled old fellow, and the rumored guest list included Donald Trump, Glenn Beck, Sarah Palin, and—at one point—Bill Clinton. Clinton was a no-show—maybe because of the inherent danger of Hillary letting Bill sleep under the same roof as Palin? Temptation is a beast! Payback is a bitch!
- The whole North Colorado thing got on the ballots in eleven counties (one of which isn't adjacent to the others, and is actually on the wrong side of the state (the northwest, while the others are on the northeast). It being an off-off year election, five of those eleven counties voted to actually leave the state and start their own.
- A Buncombe County GOP precinct chairman (he resigned

after the broadcast embarrassed the local GOP) named Don Yelton made national news (and a fool of himself) by going on Jon Stewart's *Daily Show* and making some appallingly stupid racist remarks. He was asked about the new Republican voter suppression laws being passed in NC, which he supported, and said: "When I was young, you didn't call a black a black— you called him a negra." "I had a picture one time of Obama sitting on a stump as a witch doctor, and I posted that on Facebook ... For your information, I was making fun of the white half of Obama, not the black half." "Now you have a black person using the term n*gger this and n*gger that, and it's OK for them to do it." To which, Aasif Mandvi had to ask: "You know that we can hear you, right?"

- Poll numbers of note: people who viewed the following in a positive light: GOP: 24%, Tea Party: 21%, Democrats: 39%. (NBC/*Wall St Journal*.) Also, by the time 2013 ended, Congress had slipped down to single digits (where they would pretty much remain from that point forward.) For comparison sake, here's a list of things that polled higher than the Congress: Paris Hilton, Nickelback, traffic jams (not the classic rock band), lice, Genghis Khan (posthumously, of course), root canals, cockroaches, colonoscopies, used-car salesmen, and Jar Jar Binks.

- Syria got out of control. It was in all the papers. Lefties were pissed that Obama was talking about military action; the GOP were pissed because ... maybe because they're used to being the ones wanting to bomb the shit out of places, and he beat them to it? Or because ... Rumsfeld and Cheney stopped liking Bashir Assad? Or because ... McCain talked to the "wrong" rebels? Or ... Bengazhi? Kenya? Obamacare? Well, in the end, the dire situation obviously wasn't dire enough, and the U.S. didn't get into it. Obama took it to Congress, where it didn't get the votes, in spite of the blood-lusty hawks like John McCain and his mistress Lindsey Graham, and their fluffer Kelly Ayotte. The likes of Rand

121

Paul and Alan Grayson were on the same anti-war page, which some feared might have been a sign of the apocalypse. Obama wanted to get into it, and the same GOP that were wild about Iraq suddenly balked. Maybe they feared Obama actually being able to win a war or something.

Messerism #62

One sure-fire way to make sure you never get any rest is when you mix Tea with Koch. That shit will keep you up all night.

Quotes in real time, and in the real world:

"This is the question the right has to answer: Do you want smaller government with less handouts, or do you want a low minimum wage? Because you cannot have both. If Colonel Sanders isn't going to pay the lady behind the counter enough to live on, then Uncle Sam has to. And I, for one, am getting a little tired of helping highly profitable companies pay their workers."

—Bill Maher

NINETEEN
Money Talks. Lack of Money Screams.

Did you know that Walmart, paying minimum (or as close to as possible) wages, has so many employees living in poverty that many of its employees require various forms of government aid? This costs the general tax-paying population hundreds of millions of dollars per year—on average, one million dollars—$1,000,000—in taxpayer subsidy per Walmart store. Did you know that Walmart has seen five straight quarters of falling sales and profits in the past couple of years?

Did you know that COSTCO pays an average of $21 an hour to its employees? Their starting wage is $11.50 per hour. GOP logic would tell you that, by paying so much, COSTCO would be losing money. Did you know that COSTCO has had record sales for three years in a row and posted nearly $8 billion in net sales in February 2014?

GOP logic does not add up. Especially when faced with facts.

COSTCO is proof that paying a living wage to employees actually helps their business thrive. It's good from a PR standpoint, but it also creates employee loyalty and leads to improved service to customers.

Indeed, raising the minimum wage across the board would actually be a major boost to the economy, despite the GOP naysaying. Perhaps they are not, nor should be, considered honest brokers in the discussion, since a major boost to the economy on Obama's watch might make the nation stronger (despite their constant yowling to the contrary). It also might lift people out of poverty and improve the whole supply-and-demand aspect of capitalism.

But the GOP wants everyone to believe that a raise from $7.25 per hour to $11 or more an hour would mean that companies would fear going broke, and fire a lot of people, and shoot unemployment into the sky. And that prices will jump to epic levels. A $5 Starbucks would cost

$20! Holy cow! Or soy!

In fact, prices would go up. A little. But not to perfectly match the wage jump. Why? Well, first, only a stupid CEO would drive up prices, which would drive away hordes of customers, who would cry a collective "bullshit!"

Remember how, back in 2012, Papa John (the pizza guy) went nuts over the prospect of having to provide healthcare to his underpaid employees? He threatened that it would drive up the price of his pizzas. Why, a $10- or $12-dollar pie would go up by a whopping 14 cents!

In other words, increasing the wages of employees by 50% would cause about a 1% or 2% increase in the price of stuff at Walmart, or Papa John, or the other minimum-wage places. That's because employee wages are a teeny, tiny, wee, minuscule part of their overhead, which includes such items as cost of goods (from China), shipping, bricks-and-mortar expenses like buildings and maintenance ... oh, and don't forget those executive salaries and bonuses and golden parachutes and stock dividends that bring in about $1 billion a year to the Walton family—each of them. Employee wages are like a quark in every molecule of their spending.

Looking at it historically, since the last time minimum wage went up, the prices of Papa John's pizza (and many other products on the market) rose every time oil prices increased during the Bush wars in Iraq—but didn't come back down again when oil prices fell. Oil prices, too, are a pretty small part of their overhead, but those price increases—the ones that don't benefit actual employees—don't really count, right?

Here are some real-world, real-logic facts. When people make more money, they have more money to spend. When they spend more money, the demand for goods and services increases. When demand increases, manufacturing and shipping have to increase to meet the demand. So, rather than laying off employees as a result of paying a higher wage, companies will be forced to hire more workers to step up to the demand.

Here's another: raising the minimum wage would save American taxpayers $4.6 billion from food stamp programs because citizens will no longer need to be subsidized for wages they can't survive on.

It's not simplistic, but it really is pretty simple. And it's been proven over and over and over again through history, from the Great Depression to the WWII years, to the Marshall Plan in Europe, to every recession since the 1960s, all of which we came out of by government spending, putting people back to work, and making sure the minimum wage kept up with inflation. Until the Teabaggers came along and took over the Republican Party.

A 2014 poll revealed that 69% of Republicans don't think they can live on the minimum wage. However, when asked if they support raising the minimum wage, only 37% said they would.

In July of 2014, in response to GOP intransigence about raising the minimum wage, Congressman Tim Ryan began his Minimum Wage Challenge.

He published a photo of the $154 on his desk that he and his wife had to split between them ($77 each) to make it through the week. He posted updates:

> Day one: "My wife called and let me know we had to pick up a couple of prescriptions for our new baby. Cost $24. So we are down to $130 before we even got started. My wife and children ate leftovers from a party thrown last evening in honor of our new baby. The kids ate pizza, my wife had a salad. Can't waste anything. I'm in DC and didn't want to waste too much money on just one meal at the cafeteria, so I was forced to snack on some fruit and nuts around the office today since I didn't have enough time yet to run to the store. Going to get some sardines and crackers tonight for dinner. Tomorrow or Saturday, we are going grocery shopping as a family to get food for the rest of the week.
>
> For dinner last night, I bought two cans of sardines and a box of rice crackers (cost $7). I like sardines so this was a good dinner. I picked them up at a market on Capitol Hill, so they were a little more expensive than usual. Sardines are just over a dollar in Ohio, and in DC they were over

Jeff Messer

two dollars each. (The family) ate rice pasta (cost $4) and vodka sauce (cost $3) for dinner last night.... The kids had pancakes for breakfast yesterday (cost $2) and cereal today (cost $3.50). For lunch, (they) finished off the leftover pizza, deviled eggs and watermelon from yesterday's party. I was still in DC, so I grabbed a slice of pizza for lunch at the cafeteria on Capitol Hill (cost $3). It was not a good use of money, but I was starving and rationalized it because I didn't have breakfast.... (My wife) had a $6 coupon, so she was able to buy milk and one cleaning supply from CVS. Then she signed up for another $3 coupon by giving CVS her email, which means we have an extra $3 to spend over the next couple days.

Day two: "Today, I drove back to Ohio from Washington and didn't have any food, so I picked up a Whopper from Burger King (cost $5). This was a terrible investment, honestly, and I can't remember the last fast food hamburger I ate, but I must admit, it was pretty good. I also bought a cup of coffee for the road (cost $2). Tonight I'm going to spend some time with the family, so we will tally all of the expenses up."

Day three: "Up to this point, we've spent $62. Saturday, we picked up a couple of pears, about a pound of bananas, some chocolate chip cookie mix, creamer, popcorn and a packet of Kool-aid ($12). After church today, we stopped at a farmer's stand while driving home. We got 13 ears of corn, 5 bell peppers, 6 peaches, 6 squash, 3 zucchini and a watermelon ($23). Hoping this purchase, along with some more eggs, can carry us for a couple more days. After we drove home, we had pancakes for lunch. We have allocated $25 - $30 for transportation. Around $30 for the next four days."

Day five: Over the weekend, my family and I attended a

birthday picnic for a close friend who turned 85 years old, which saved us one meal. For dinner last night, we picked up some bratwurst (cost $6) and cooked some corn we bought. It was a nice dinner and gave us some leftovers for the next day or two.

This week my family and I experienced firsthand why $7.25 an hour is not a livable wage, which is why today unfortunately brought us to the end of our budget. My stepdaughter is beginning summer camp and had a music lesson. These expenses left $4.50 for purchases.

One thing this showed us is that the extra money people make will get invested back into their families. Do minimum-wage families make enough money to eat? Yes, many can make it work. But the real question is—what can't they do when living on minimum wage?"

Along the way, Representative Ryan pointed out that in 1968 the minimum wage was $1.60. Adjusted for inflation, that would be $10.86 today. Some other useful facts about minimum wage:

Federal Poverty Level for a Family of Two:	$15,730
Average Minimum Wage Salary:	$15,080

The value of the minimum wage as of 2013 was $4.87, adjusted for inflation using the Consumer Price Index; that's on par with 1991, when it was $4.90.

How many hours would you have to work at minimum wage to afford rent?

According to the National Low Income Housing Coalition, as of 2013, no minimum wage worker in *any* state in the USA can afford a two-bedroom apartment at Fair Market Rent, while working a standard 40-hour work week, without paying more than 30% of their income.

Work-hours needed in select states to afford an apartment:

North Carolina:	78
Florida:	98
Virginia:	114
West Virginia:	68 (lowest)
Maryland:	135
Colorado:	89
Montana:	69
California:	128
Texas:	92
Minnesota:	89
New York:	139 (highest)
New Jersey:	137
Illinois:	82
Georgia:	84
Washington DC:	132

Some good news, however, came to thirteen states that raised their minimum wage effective January 1, 2014. They are:

Arizona
Colorado
Connecticut
Florida
Missouri
Montana
New Jersey
New York
Ohio
Oregon
Rhode Island
Vermont
Washington

Eleven other states are also considering raising minimum wage on their own. North Carolina is NOT one of them.

Statistics from the AFL-CIO show that raising wages to a "living wage" of only $25,000 per year (as opposed to the current $15,000 for minimum wage), would lift 750,000 people out of poverty, increase the GDP by $11.8 billion, and create as many as 100,000 new jobs.

I have seen numbers out there that indicate that a simple raise to $10.10 an hour for minimum wage would lift as many as 5 million people out of poverty, though I wonder about that number, in comparison the AFL-CIO numbers above, since $10.10 would only raise the pre-tax pay to just over $21,000 per year. (Mind you, if you are used to struggling on $15,000, a bump to $21,000 would seem like living the high life).

The popular Internet meme of $11 per hour would translate to around $23,000 a year. To achieve the AFL-CIO number, the per-hour wage would have to be slightly above $12.

So take it as you will. Any way you take it though, it is a great boost for people, and the economy. And, of course, you have to temper that with things like the variance in cost of living from city to city, and region to region.

And keep in mind that the above breakdowns are actually a more detailed conversation about wages and the real numbers than any member of Congress has had or has even been willing to entertain. Well, almost any:

The hell you say? Quotable reality:

"If we started in 1960 and we said that, as productivity goes up, then the minimum wage is going to go up the same ... the minimum wage today would be about $22 an hour. So, my question: with the minimum wage of $7.25 per hour, what happened to the other $14? It certainly didn't go to the workers."

—Senator Elizabeth Warren

"Today, the United States is number one in billionaires, number one in corporate profits, number one in CEO salaries, number one in childhood poverty, and number one in income and wealth inequality in the industrialized world."

—Senator Bernie Sanders

Jeff Messer

"No one who works full time in America should have to raise a family in poverty. It's time to raise the minimum wage."
—President Barack Obama

"That's not even enough to raise a family."*
—NC Governor Pat McCrory

(McCrory was talking about teacher pay of $31,000 per year—twice the minimum wage and, according to him, still too little to live on. But his GOP refused to raise the minimum wage in general in the state.)

*It's not enough to pay off the student loans teachers incur as t hey get their degrees, either.

Messerism #71

Only one color matters in politics these days. It isn't black or white. It's green. If you've got the green, you can be one of them. If you don't, you can bet that they are going to do everything they can to make sure you never will.

TWENTY
THE (MIS-)EDUCATION OF PUPPET PAT

There may not have been a bigger hot-button issue in NC in recent years than the debate over funding education. In fact, there has never been a time in my life when it was not widely known that the state's teachers were underpaid and generally disrespected. And there has never been a time when I have not known just about everyone to believe that teachers deserve better than our politicians give them.

So, the education problem is a pretty nonpartisan, long-term issue. Both parties have let teachers down. Repeatedly.

But during the 1990s and 2000s, the Legislature did make an erratic effort to improve the lot of teachers here. They gradually moved pay rates closer and closer to the national average, but the last increase for teachers in the state was in 2008. When the Great Bush Recession hit and the world's economy crashed in 2008-09, NC teacher pay had just about reached the median for all states, at which point it pretty much froze (along with everything else):

Naturally enough, in 2013, with a new governor in town and a full GOP-controlled General Assembly (whom I happily think of as General Ass) firmly in control, public and media attention turned to what policy would emerge concerning the state education system. Soon, though, a lot of people lost hope of things getting any better, despite some flowery talk.

First, the universities were targeted. The UNC system had lost $414 million in funding in 2011 (before McCrory took office, but after the GOP had the Legislature). They cut an additional $66 million in 2013, with a two-year budget plan to cut yet another $500 million from public education, and a cut to textbook funding to the tune of $77.4 million. That was right in line with their massive $700 million income-tax cuts for the wealthiest residents in the state. Then, General Ass took aim at secondary education.

Here are some points of interest to help frame the conversation more fully:

Average teacher pay in the U.S., 2012-2013: $55,418
Average teacher pay in NC, 2012-2013: $45,938
                                (82.9% of U.S. average)
NC Rank: 46

Source: NC Dept. of Public Instruction

According to the National Center for Education Statistics, since the 1999-2000 school year, teacher pay had fallen by 14.7%.

The numbers spoke for themselves, and so did the public mood. People were up in arms about the way General Ass had treated schools in 2011-12, and how in 2013-14 it was screwing education at all levels—including taking $10 million of tax money for private-school vouchers. Smelling blood in the water—and finally waking up to the fact that it was their own blood they were smelling—the Governor and Legislature rolled into 2014 with some of their best proposals yet. Typically, they offered help with one hand while delivering a sucker punch with the other. They can't help themselves: it's in their DNA.

Here's how they decided to act: loudly offer pay raises for new teachers, and quietly eliminate career status and job protections for veterans. Increase overall spending, but cut spending on a per-capita basis (since the school population was growing much faster than funding increases). Classroom size would increase under the new plans, and the number of teaching assistants would be reduced.

So early in 2014 Puppet Pat, Phil Berger, Thom Tillis and Lt. Governor Dan Forest (who seems desperate to keep a low profile among the out-of-control circus of Stephen King *It* clowns) rolled out an "ambitious" package of a 14% pay raise for new teachers, spread over two years—with increases as little as 0.3% for 30-year veterans. Starting pay for teachers in 2013-14 was just under $31,000. The new plan would give them a $2,200 raise in 2014-15, and an additional $2,000 the following year. It would take fifteen years for a new teacher to reach $40,000 in annual salary.

To a lot of people it seemed a clear attempt to pit new against old, drive out the more experienced teachers to make way for new ones, who would get a pay bump but still earn less than their more experienced counterparts. Their plan was like a sadistic desire to see teacher groups squaring off, veterans v. newbies, those with M.Eds. against BAs—sort of gladiator lite.

In a way, it worked—if you consider backfiring a forward motion.

On two separate occasions during 2014, Texas school systems took out ads in North Carolina newspapers, openly recruiting teachers and soon-to-be-graduated teachers to be with offers of better pay and a clear promise of more respect.

Texass. Just saying.

In the spring of 2014, teacher Sarah Wiles wrote a scathing email to the General Ass.

> From: Sarah Wiles
>
> Sent: Tuesday, May 06, 2014 6:47 PM
>
> Every year there is a debate on teacher compensation. This is only exacerbated during election years. However, nothing happens. As a sixth year teacher, I have only seen a pay increase once (and then again after plunging myself into debt by earning my Masters in Education). I have attended rallies, joined NCAE, petitioned, and worn red (or blue and white, or whatever color of the rainbow I was required to wear to "show my support'). Nothing ever changes, except my wardrobe. So, that brings me to this one request: leave me alone.
>
> I am so tired of being lied to about how important I am and how valuable I am. I am also sick and tired of politicians making my profession the center of attention and paying it lip-service by visiting a school, kneeling next to a child, shaking my hand and thanking me, telling the nightly news that I deserve a raise, and then proceeding to speak through

the budget that I am not worth it. If you aren't going to do anything, and you know nothing will change, just leave me alone. I would rather be ignored than disrespected.

And on the topic of disrespect, our salary is disrespectful. I tutor my own students for free four days a week after school until I have to go to my next job. I tutor outside of school for pay about fifteen hours a week, and that includes weekends. I also babysit. And I manage pools and teach pool operator classes. And, I currently have an application for summer school being reviewed. I get home at eight pm, spend a half an hour with my husband, answer parent emails, fall asleep, and am back at work at seven am the next morning. I have become very accustomed to being disrespected. My students know that no one cares about education because they frequently ask me why I ever made the decision to become a teacher. Honestly, I am running out of answers. Do not misunderstand or misconstrue what I am saying as apathy for my students (I love them more than most adults), but I can no longer defend that North Carolina cares about education because they are not willing to pay for it. It's a lie and everyone knows it.

I know that you all will continue talking about how important teachers are and weaving those wonderful words that tax payers love to hear from the people who are "leading" them that make them believe that it isn't all about the bottom line and that you care about their kids and the public education system. But, I am calling your bluff. If you continue to do nothing even though you can do something, you should be ashamed. I am embarrassed for you. I am embarrassed by you. And, save for my students, I am embarrassed by being a teacher in North Carolina, the doormat of society.

Sarah Wiles, M.A.Ed.

Pretty insightful, and right to the point. Now, a smart politician would know to just ignore it, and hope it will go away. Of course, no one ever accused too many members of the General Ass of being smart. And Representative David Curtis just couldn't help himself, but reply to Sarah. After all, he was clearly in the right. He's a man. He's smarter. He's a "leader."

Here's David Curtis's email reply:

> From: Sen. David Curtis
>
> Date: May 12, 2014 at 9:46:57
>
> Dear Sarah,
>
> I have given your e-mail titled "I am embarrassed to confess: I am a teacher" some thought, and these are my ideas. A teacher has an incredible influence on students—for good or for bad. My teachers, coaches, and Boy Scout leaders had a great influence on my decision to go to college which was not a family tradition. My concern is that your students are picking up on your attitude toward the teaching profession. Since you naturally do not want to remain in a profession of which you are ashamed, here are my suggestions for what you should tell your potential new private sector employer:
>
> 1. You expect to make a lot more than you made as a teacher because everyone knows how poorly compensated teachers are.
>
> 2. You expect at least eight weeks paid vacation per year because that is what the taxpayers of North Carolina gave you back when you were a poorly compensated teacher.
>
> 3. You expect a defined contribution retirement plan that will guarantee you about $35,000 per year for life after working 30 years even if you live to be 104 years old. Your employer will need to put about $16,000 per year into your retirement plan each year combined with your $2,000 contribution for the

next 30 years to achieve this benefit. If he objects, explain to him that a judge has ruled that the taxpayers of North Carolina must provide this benefit to every public school teacher. Surely your new employer wants to give better benefits than the benefits you received as a poorly compensated teacher.

4. Your potential employer may tell you that he has heard that most North Carolina workers make less than the national average because we are a low cost-of-living- state, private sector workers making 87% of the national average and teachers making 85% of the national average. Tell him that may be true, but to keep that confidential because the teachers union has convinced parents that teachers are grossly under compensated based on a flawed teachers union survey of teacher pay.

I support the teacher pay raise but am very concerned that the teachers union has successfully presented to the public a deceptive view of total teacher compensation that is simply not consistent with the facts.

Sincerely,

Senator David Curtis

Prick much, Davey? At least he wrote "sincerely" at the end. Shame on anyone who votes to re-elect this clown.

Almost five weeks past the deadline for passing a budget, and at the cost of nearly $1 million dollars to pay for the over-extended "short session," in late July of 2014, General Ass finally agreed on a 7% raise.

New Rank: 32 out of 50

That 7% was not easy to come to, and it showed internal fraying in the General Ass. The GOP controlled both House and Senate, yet the funding for education so divided them that they could not get the budget passed and get out of town to campaign and fund-raise for the upcoming mid-terms.

It went something like this:

The House wants a 5% pay raise for teachers, with tenure protections. The Senate wants an 11% pay raise, but no tenure protections. Teachers' assistants cut back for Grade 3 and up.

They finally settled on 7%, which did not appease the too-smart-not-to-see-though-the-bullshit educators, who had taken to staging massive protests and rallies on their own, as well as within the massive Moral Mondays movement.

Rodney Ellis, president of the NC Association of Educators, told the Associated Press in early 2014, "It does seem highly unlikely that it's a coincidence that this year, we are going to the polls, and this year there's finally going to be an effort to do something for teacher salaries."

Here's the result of the NC teacher pay raise, by the numbers:
- Of the $21-billion-dollar budget, the pay raise accounts for $282 million, or 1.34%
- $700 million given in tax breaks to upper-bracket tax-payers in the state this year, and $5.3 billion to the same class over five years
- Adjusted for inflation, teachers now earn, on average, $4,212 less than they did in 2008-09, before the pay freeze
- $76 million dollars was cut from the UNC system, depriving colleges
- U.S. average teacher pay: $56,130
- NC average teacher pay: $43,517 (77.5% of U.S. average)

The new "pay raise" applies to teachers who have been working less than five years, including new teachers just starting out. Veteran teachers are not given a raise. And, it should be noted that veteran teachers in NC, who have been on the job for as much as twenty years, are already making less than the U.S. average for teacher pay.

Shopping for good schools

Despite having a first-class university system, secondary education is North Carolina has long been underfunded, forced to beg for scraps.

Here's an illustration, in two real-life anecdotes.

True story #1: In 2010, on the "meet the teacher" day for my son's second-grade class, the teacher's assistant handed out a three-page stapled list of things that the classroom needed. The handout asked parents who could afford to do so to please purchase extra items (listed) and bring them to class. After all, responsible parents want to make sure that the classroom their child is in is a success.

I noticed that the handout was printed from an email, not typed on its own. As such, page 3 of the hand out was almost entirely blank, and just had that annoying line of type that you get at the end of an email when you print it.

Irony? The handout included asking for parents to purchase and provide an additional ream of copy paper.

Sigh.

True story #2: I was in a Target store a couple of weeks later and noticed that the entire "Back To School" department was marked on clearance, up to 75% off. I filled a shopping cart with stacks of pencils, glue sticks, spiral notebooks, rulers, etc. I paid around $25 total for the purchase, loaded it into a giant tub, and took it to the classroom the next day.

The class shared with other second-grade teachers, and some of the supplies lasted the entire school year.

I don't tell this tale to get pats on the back. I tell it to (hopefully) inspire others to go and do the same thing.

When in line at the check-out counter, the three people who came up behind me all made positive comments, assuming I was a teacher. When I told them I was a parent, and when they saw that the full cart of items rang up to just $25 dollars, they were all amazed, and said they would do likewise the next day. I hope that word spread.

I do this every year, when I can. However, sadly, one year, I posted online that I was doing this, and I got berated by a self-identified liberal, who said I was not helping the big picture, but rather helping the politicians to keep cutting corners and ignoring the education system's needs. And while I agree on some level, I am just not willing to let my kid's school suffer to prove a bigger point. I would rather just elect better people, and then hold them accountable once elected.

Newer rank: 51 out of 50

That's the number WalletHub.com came up with for North Carolina's rank among "best and worst states for teachers." That's right. Fifty-first out of fifty states. They counted the District of Columbia, too. Remember how Arkansans used to say, "Thank God for Mississippi?" Well, Mississippi ranked 50th. Guess what Mississippians are saying now?

Writers right quote:

Public education does not exist for the benefit of the students or the benefit of their parents. It exists for the benefit of social order.

We have discovered as a species that it is useful to have an educated population. You do not need to be a student or have a child who is a student to benefit from the public education. Every second of your life, you benefit from public education.

So let me explain why I like to pay taxes for schools, even though I don't personally have a kid in school: it's because I don't like living in a country with a bunch of stupid people.

—John Green, author of *The Fault in Our Stars*

Messerism #61

I had no idea that when all that right-wing talk about wanting to "take America back" was so literal, because it sure as hell sounds like they want to take us back to the 1950s at least, and the 1850s at worst. Between Marty McFly and Dr. Sam Beckett, I would hope we can see the possible dangers in such a time-travel aspiration.

TWENTY-ONE
VOTER WRONGS, FROM THE RIGHT

Remember Jim Crow? It was in all the papers. You know, for those who could pass a literacy test at the polls in order to vote.

We thought we had left those days behind us, though it took some forceful maneuvering and legislation to level the decidedly un-level playing field, as refereed by the dominant white folk in the South who just didn't cotton to the notion of those darker-skinned types getting to have a say in the outcomes of elections.

Well, in 2013, the U.S. Supreme Court, in its 5-4 supreme wisdom, decided that such protections and laws were no longer necessary. After all, we had a black man in the White House. Surely we were now a fully evolved nation. Well, except for when it comes to Latinos, same-sex couples, and the poor. But, hey: What are you looking for over here? Life, liberty, and the pursuit of happiness? What do you think this is? A place where all are created equally? Geez!

It is a sad day when the Bush-league majority of the Supreme Court either decides to be manipulative in the racial divide, tipping scales backward in some deep southern states, or they are too damned dumb to realize that some folks, in some places, are not past the old racism—and that for the most part those are the same "some places" that were covered for fifty years by the Voting Rights Act. You know, the solid South, the reactionary, secessionist, rebel-flag, former-slave-states South. Maybe someone should have shown them some Google images of all those racist signs at recent Tea Party rallies.

And almost at once, after the Supreme Court struck down provisions that gave such protections, some states—I give you three guesses which ones—moved swiftly to take advantage. (Some, like Ohio and Indiana, weren't in the Old South, but they're vying to be the first among equals in the "new old South"). Not wanting to be outdone, North Carolina broke land-speed records in rolling back voting rights in the state more vehemently and comprehensively than anywhere else—even Texass.

This did not sit well with a lot of people. Of all races and backgrounds.

It's almost like General Ass realized that what they are doing legislatively was so vile, and so poisonous, and so immoral, that a massive voter pushback would be coming their way that will send them all packing. So, if they are to keep their power, they needed to make damn sure that all those angry people that they're screwing over won't, or can't, show up to vote. And if they do, maybe their votes can be made to not count.

Welcome to the new NC.

Of course, the state GOP had already been working hard to shut down voters in other ways. Namely places like college campuses, when huge pockets of away-from-home young folks gathered in their Liberal Arts huddles to do all sorts of wild, fun, youthful things. Like vote for progress.

How do they stop those pockets of (D)-voting youth from having an impact? How about ... make it illegal for their parents to claim tax deductions for them, as parents, unless their kids vote at the family's home address, hopefully out of state? How about ... close polling places near campuses, so that students have to drive, ride a bus, or walk at least a mile on a road with no sidewalks to get to one small rural poll serving 10,000 students? How about ... split a campus with new district lines so that half the students are in one district, half in another—but don't tell them, and then demand their votes not be counted if they voted in the wrong half. How about ... make it so that student ID cards, even those issued by a NC state university, no longer count as valid IDs to cast a ballot?

And what about those folks out there who are old, or poor, and most likely don't have any current state ID cards like a driver's license? Got to do something about them too! Pesky old, poor people—who are most likely to want to vote, and don't like cuts to their grandchildren's schools, and want to protect the Medicaid they rely on. And who like to vote early because they don't drive anymore, and they can't wait on line for hours with their walkers or wheelchairs, and they need to vote when the weather's warm enough. Well, how about ... cut the number of days for early voting in half, and limit it to weekdays, and ...

And, hey, that takes care of all those working folks who got big tax increases instead of mega-tax cuts from General Ass this year, too. You know, people who can't afford take time off on a Tuesday to go vote. (Or aren't allowed to take time off to vote, especially if they're working people and Democrats who work for Art Pope's Republican-owned discount chain.)

And, as a bonus, you throw some tire spikes under all those African American church buses that take busloads of their members out early to cast ballots. Let's end Early Voting on the final Sunday before the election; that gets them off the voting rolls without even a poll tax.

It became a national and international embarrassment as headlines proclaimed the regressive actions of the twisted NC GOP. Many pointed out that North Carolina had passed laws that took the state all the way back to the days of those Jim Crow laws.

A huge black eye for the Tarheel State. Of course, the GOP in charge seemed to not be bothered by all the talk and attention. They simply didn't care that they looked like a bunch of backward-looking, semi-hick, fully racist bunch of greedy bastards. After all, if they got their way, they would stay in power, and eventually not have to even pretend to care about the voters.

Some laws went into immediate effect, while the crucial law about requiring all voters to have a state-issued ID to vote would not be in effect until the 2016 election.

Needless to say, lawsuits followed the swift-moving maneuvering.

And on December 12, 2013, a federal court ruled that a trial over the sweeping voter suppression laws will be held in 2015—after the 2014 elections.

The ACLU, the ACLU of North Carolina Legal Foundation, and the Southern Coalition for Social Justice's lawsuit targeted provisions in the law that eliminates a week of early voting, prohibits "out of precinct" voting and ends same-day registration, stating that such things would unduly burden the right to vote and discriminate against African American voters. That would be a violation of the equal protections clause in the Constitution and the Voting Rights Act of 1965.

The League of Women Voters also brought suit, citing that a number of North Carolinians would face substantial hardship under the new law.

A lot of forces were rising up against these new moves. And the Moral Monday movement would take up the cause, as well.

So, what on earth would the GOP have to say in their defense? How would they respond?

In April of 2014, House Speaker Thom Tillis and Senate Leader Phil Berger dropped a bombshell to end all bombshells when they released a joint statement concerning a scale of voter fraud that, if believed, would be the most significant in the history of all of democracy.

The discovery of this massive voter fraud came through the NC State Board of Elections, whose initial findings were presented to the Joint Legislative Elections Oversight Committee.

The data takes into account numbers from only twenty-eight states that participated in the 2014 Interstate Crosscheck. The other twenty-two states that didn't participate could actually add to the numbers that were revealed.

Here's what they boldly proclaimed:

- In NC 765 voters were found with an exact match of first and last name, date of birth, and last four digits of Social Security numbers, who were registered in NC and in another state, and voted in NC and the other state in the 2012 general election
- 35,750 voters were discovered to have the same first and last name and date of birth, and were registered in NC and another state, and voted in both states in the 2012 general election
- 155,692 voters were found with the same first and last name, date of birth, and last four digits of Social Security Number, and were registered in NC and another state, and whose latest date of registration or voter activity did not take place in NC

Additionally, there was an audit conducted of death records from the Department of Health and Human Services that revealed:

- 81 dead people who voted after they died
- 13,416 dead voters were on the voter rolls in October 2013
- 50,000 new death records that had not previously been provided to the State Board of Elections

I know that's a lot of numbers to absorb, but I'll do my best to try and decipher the data and prove how incredibly irresponsible it was for Tillis and Berger to latch onto it as the proof of voter fraud and justification for the new voting laws that stood to harm so many. Well, so many who are not already elected GOP officials, looking to keep their cushy jobs, or ascend to some other higher paid cushier job.

The findings that they were touting only existed because of a new election reform law that had been passed by the General Assembly a year earlier. It called on the Board of Elections to improve the accuracy of voter registration lists and combat potential fraud by cross-checking with voting records in other states.

Now, first and foremost, it should be pointed out that the numbers being presented are from the 2012 general election. And, while that's the election that returned President Obama to office for four more years, there is a far more embarrassing aspect to the GOP of NC pointing at 2012 and crying foul. After all, it was that very election that brought the GOP back to full power in NC for the first time in over a century.

So, in their infinite wisdom, they were calling into question an election that allowed them to seize power and go bananas on the state, in a revenge tale that Quentin Tarantino would find unsettling.

Sources matter

It's important to know where the "fraud" numbers came from.

According to the Institute for Southern Studies, the cross-check of North Carolina voters "was conducted by the office of Kris Kobach, the controversial Secretary of State in Kansas." Kobach claims that in 2013, among the twenty-eight states whose voting records they accessed, "the program flagged a staggering five million records of people whose names and date of birth appeared to match."

But there's no evidence of any actual fraud. Kobach's office was unable to provide "any evidence of a single instance in which the ... data had led to an actual legal charge of voter fraud." It does point to fourteen cases "referred for prosecution," but not one single case where charges were brought or any voter convicted.

When Colorado used the program in 2013, Republican Secretary of State Scott Gessler announced it had identified seventeen cases of alleged fraud. A few months later the Boulder County District Attorney's office dismissed every one of them, saying none involved actual fraud and that they were all "politically motivated."

Beyond that, and the origin of these supposed "voter-fraud" numbers, here are some pretty clear ways to understand them.

First: Among the 319 million who inhabit this nation, more than one might have the same name—and even the same birthday. Ever Google yourself with just your name? Oh, look—there are "25 professionals named Jeff Messer, who use LinkedIn to exchange information"—and probably countless non-professionals, or professional Jeff Messers who don't use LinkedIn, but might be on Facebook, or Google+, or Twitter. And some who use all those platforms, or several of them. How many? Scores? Hundreds? A few thousand? Who knows?

And "Messer" isn't even in the Top 100 most common U.S. surnames. Not even the top 1,000! I mean, it's below such all-American names—and targets for Republican purging—as Garcia, Martinez, Rodriguez, Hernandez, Lopez, Gonzalez, Perez, Sanchez, Rivera, Torres, Ramirez, Diaz ... to say nothing of McCrory, Tillis, Berger, or Moffitt.

Second: North Carolina's population includes a lot of people who have moved here from other states, or maintain dual residences, so it's not uncommon to find a large number of people who live here, and, oh, let's say, Florida. Many others relocate or retire here and simply don't bother to contact the Board of Elections in their former state and say, "Take me off the rolls."

And young people, too: there are colleges in other states that appeal to students from our state, and colleges here that attract students from elsewhere. Many of them might cross state lines to go to college, or transfer from, say U. Kentucky to UNC Asheville. And forget to "unregister" when they move. Thereby producing two locations for one person.

Third: Eighty-one voters whose votes are counted after they died probably voted absentee. Many people (far more Republicans than Democrats, by the numbers; and far more old and wealthy—also skewing Republican—than young and poor) get absentee ballots and make sure to send them in during the weeks before the election. And some of them die before the first Tuesday in November. But their ballots still get counted on Election Day. AFTER THEY DIED!!! Do you think we should eliminate all those dead Republican votes? Hmmmm.

Fourth: Whenever a loved one dies, obviously the first thing that grieving family members think is: "We better call the Election Board and tell them that Mom won't be voting anymore." Not. People don't do that. As a result, there are probably thousands upon thousands of late lamented people whose families simply don't think about having them removed from the roles. That number in NC could easily reach the 13,416 figure—given that 81,798 people died in NC in 2012. When you consider that they found 50,000 death records that the Elections Board had never seen, I think it's self-evident.

Finally, there's that number of 765 voters who have exact name, birthday, and Social Security number matches in NC and another state. That would be worth pondering, if there were any evidence at all (see sidebar about Kobach above) that they voted in both places. But, for real, there's not. Not one iota of evidence. No proof, no leads, no evidence.

So I have to wonder: If they have such detailed information, and it's real and credible, and was announced in April of 2014, why is that there are not 765 people being tried for voter fraud? After all, Tillis and Berger clearly indicate that they have the names, and clearly know where and how to find them at one of their two listed addresses.

Why have we not heard of the Trial of the Century for voter fraud? As a matter of fact, why haven't we heard any more about this massive voter-fraud issue since the Berger-Tillis announcement in April?

Well, maybe it's because Democrats really aren't sophisticated or smart or crooked enough to try to commit voter fraud. Maybe because they believe in Democracy and think it would be wrong to steal extra votes. Maybe because they're not Republicans like …:

- the Scott Walker supporter in Wisconsin who got busted in June of 2014 on thirteen counts of voter fraud, after he voted a dozen times in five elections between 2011 and 2012, using his name as well as his son's name and his girlfriend's son's name—and then claimed a form of temporary amnesia

- the young Republican contractor in Virginia who threw scores of voter registration forms in the trash in October of 2012, as witnessed by a local store manager

- the Bassett County, Virginia, GOP supporter who pleaded guilty to thirty-six counts of voter fraud and perjury, after he attempted to help Newt Gingrich get enough signatures to get on the primary ballot there

- the Florida cases against Strategic Allied Consulting, a GOP-hired vendor, in which investigations found at least eleven voter registration forms that were of questionable authenticity. Two cases were closed for lack of evidence, but there were three additional cases opened after the 2012 election.

- the two Republicans who wanted to prove how easy it was to vote in two states, back in November 2012—and were arrested

- the four staffers for Michigan Republican Thaddeus McCotter indicted in August 2012 for submitting over 1,500 "forged or falsified" signatures in what the Michigan Attorney General (also a Republican) called "blatant and disgraceful" behavior

- Indiana's Republican Secretary of State, Charlie White, who was found guilty on six counts of voter fraud, theft and perjury in a February 2012 Indiana jury trial

It turns out that most voter fraud is apparently committed by Republicans and their supporters, including the Diebold voting-machine owner who told a Republican business meeting that his job was to make sure George W. Bush was elected president (see p. 219 for more details).

Yet despite being caught red-handed over and over again, the GOP has yelled the loudest and the longest about voter fraud committed by Democrats. They never, ever, ever manage to find any evidence that it happens—at least since Chicago in 1960. Even a comprehensive, five-year, nationwide investigation (conducted from 2002-07 by the Bush Justice Department led by hyper-partisan Attorney General Alberto Gonzalez and pushed by White House political operative Karl Rove) found virtually no evidence of any real voter fraud. The probe led to 120 prosecutions and eighty-six convictions—many of which were of paroled felons who mistakenly thought they could vote after serving their time, but were still prohibited if they were on probation.

But if Tillis and Berger are to be believed, there are at least 765 conclusive, easily convictable cases that have been uncovered in NC (and at least one other state, associated with each instance).

I'm waiting for the trials to begin.

REAL voter fraud numbers

The Washington Post released the following in the summer of 2014:
- Since 2000, there have been over 1,000,000,000—that's one billion—ballots cast in the United States in elections
- Alleged voter fraud in that time that might have been prevented by voter ID laws: 31
- That's a rate of .000000031% over thirteen years

Messerism #88

When it comes to voting, turnout is embarrassing low, which serves to help validate the wrong-headed legislators and keep them moving forward along their agenda, or the agenda of their funders. They think that if people don't care enough or aren't upset enough to show up and vote them out, then they must be justified. And if voters aren't paying attention, or holding them accountable, it doesn't hurt their feelings. Why? Because there are any number of special interests with fat checkbooks, standing there ready to pay them all the attention they could want or need.

Which can often lead to:

Messerism #89

Too many smart people think they are above participating in the process, and use the mantra that "my vote doesn't count." They somehow think that the act of not voting is the ultimate act of defiance, when in fact, it is simply waving the white flag of surrender.

TIGHT-FITTING NATIONAL BRIEFS #5
GIVE ME YOUR STATS, STAT!

Every year, American taxpayers pay Congress more than $93,000,000 in salary alone. In 2014, they worked fewer than 125 days. If you aren't voting, you're letting a small number of people hire the people that you're helping pay to do things you may not like.

Every one of the forty-one elected Republican senators blocked a raise in the minimum wage. Yet they will each receive a $2,800 cost-of-living adjustment effective January 1, 2015.

Left, right, and center-left

Salon.com compiled polling data from various American polling organizations describing the policy preferences of the American people over the last year. Their findings would seem to contradict the popular theory that America is a center-right nation:

Support fairer distribution of U.S. wealth:	59%
Oppose cuts to Social Security and Medicaid:	69%
Support minimum-wage increase to $10.10 an hour:	71%
Support same-sex marriage:	59%
Support a woman's right to choose:	54%
Support legalizing marijuana:	58%
Support pathway to citizenship:	68%
Support universal background checks on gun purchases:	81%
Believe climate change is a serious issue:	73%

These numbers actually support the theory that we are more of a center-left nation.

Jeff Messer

GOP legislative "action"

Forty-two senators (41 GOP, and 1 Democrat) blocked a bill that would limit tax breaks for U.S. companies that move operations overseas to avoid taxes and exploit cheap labor abroad (summer 2014).

All Senate Republicans blocked a bill that would allow 25 million Americans dealing with student loan debt to refinance at lower rates. Majority Leader Harry Reid voted with them as a procedural move that would allow him to reintroduce it later (summer 2014).

Climate Change update, Asheville bureau

January 2014 rolled in, on a cold wind. Or rather, a Polar Vortex.

Ah, the Polar Vortex. With it, there was some snow, but for the most part, 2014 opened with sub-zero temperatures blanketing most of the region. Low-temperature records were set. Days on end saw wind-chill temps far below zero.

Of course, the ignorant masses of asses brayed on and on about how this surely put an end to the whole "global warming" thing.

Winter set individual day records for low temperatures, and snowfall in places like Atlanta and Raleigh created chaos on the Internet, as traffic and traffic controllers and persons who are ill-equipped to handle such conditions (like highway-clearing crews) embarrassed themselves in all manner of traffic jams on icy roads.

Special appreciation shout-out for whoever took a much-seen photo of I-40 near Raleigh, where mystifyingly a car appeared to be on fire amid the multitude of stalled, wrecked, or abandoned vehicles—and the person Photoshopped into the picture an Imperial Walker from *The Empire Strikes Back* seeming to be firing upon said burning car.

REAL LIFE UPDATE #5

On February 1, 2014, I married my girlfriend of over four years. Kelli and I met about a year after our first marriages had ended, and found a surprising connection that quickly led from one thing to another, and it became quite serious.

For years I had a reputation for consistently dating younger women, one after another. I got older, but my dates stayed young. It was hardly the best reputation to carry into adulthood. So, I slowed down, had a kid, got married, got derailed, then got rewarded!

Kelli is walking perfection. She is a former Miss Asheville (1996), and a professional musician with a seminary degree (which keeps me straight when I try to cite scriptural contradictions from the right wing on my radio show.)

I once joked that I was married to a hot seminarian, which is exactly as dirty—and as true—as it sounds.

Our adventures together helped us both learn that there are second chances in life. And I learned that I had made a huge mistake by dating so many young women. It took me 'til I was forty to realize that women are better at absolutely everything, and so much sexier, after thirty. What a revelation! What good advice for other guys like me!

Anyway…

The wedding was a short ceremony with her two children and my one, and a small gathering of our nearest and dearest friends and family. The vows, which we wrote, were a sweet, sincere, and somewhat amusing homage to the fun we had found with each other over the four years of our relationship.

A quick honeymoon included a sweet suite in Charlotte with a hot tub in the bedroom, from which we watched the beatdown that was the Superbowl. And now I'm a married man again!

Jeff Messer

TWENTY-TWO
GIVE A POLLUTE, NOT A HOOT!

Folks near Eden in northeastern NC and across the border in Virginia got a bonus on Superbowl Sunday, February 2, 2014, as a massive coal-ash facility dumped tons of toxic filth into the Dan River.

Brought to you by Duke Energy!

Complete & Utter Coincidence: Governor Pat McCrory spent over a quarter of a century in the employ of Duke Energy, and had a small fortune in Duke stock in his portfolio. (He had lied about owning it on two ethics disclosure forms, and then secretly sold it sometime after the spill—and after he was asked about his investment in the company).

Move along, move along, folks. Nothing to see there, look this way.

This disaster came on the heels of the horror story in West Virginia, where a relatively small chemical spill contaminated a major river that crippled a number of counties by rendering their water supply unusable: 300,000 people were suddenly without clean water to drink or bathe in. They couldn't even cook with it, as boiling water didn't eliminate the contaminants. Needless to say, businesses were also brought to a standstill for the weeks that it took to get things cleaned up. And the company quickly declared bankruptcy, and even more quickly tried to get out of town. The sad irony is that a photo that appeared online showed the site responsible for the spill—and in view right across the river was a billboard preaching about how regulations hurt jobs.

The Duke coal-ash spill into the Dan River was not as severe, but it did set people on edge across the state when it became more widely known that there are some thirty-one similar coal ash facilities within the state (a few near Asheville) and that a similar calamity could happen quite easily at any of them.

It didn't help that, days into the spill, officials sent a camera probe into the pipes around the site, where they discovered a startling number of leaks through which arsenic was leaking into the waterway.

It also didn't help that the time stamp on the camera footage showed that they had known about it for a number of days before acknowledging that arsenic was seeping out, along with the coal ash.

When all was said and done, a massive cleanup was ordered, and a major re-evaluation was made of all the state's aging and potentially defective coal-ash facilities. Then costs were given for all of the required fixes, and Duke Energy officials promptly announced that the shareholders (the governor among them) would not be picking up the tab to clean up the mess and get things in order. Not on your life. The entire cost of the cleanup—and beyond—would fall solely on the ratepayers.

This is how it goes when you get a wild right-wing, deregulation-happy, GOP-filled Tea-tastic, totalitarian regime in power. The Department of Energy and Natural Resources? The Department of Health? The Department of Consumer Affairs? All part of the same team.

Nobody in power was interested in doing the right thing, and no-one had the power to call them out on it. And the cries of foul from the public were openly ignored, and surely mockingly laughed at behind closed doors. It's kind of like that "quiet room" where Mitt Romney and his (self-)important cronies are so fond of doing the people's business—McCrory, the mini-Mitt.

Messerism #117

Last time I checked, we have only one planet to live on, and since we mothballed NASA, we're not out there looking for a backup. So why is it that corporations don't seem to think we should stop poisoning the planet in which we live? Hate to break it to them, but endless stacks of money in off-shore banking locations are not going to help them breathe any easier than the rest of us when we're all choking on what's left of the atmosphere. Rich and dead is still dead.

TWENTY-THREE
RALEIGH & GOMORRAH: REAL MORALITY COMES TO THE CAPITAL

One week after my wedding, I was up at 4 a.m. to catch one of half a dozen buses to Raleigh. Flurries of snow fell as I randomly picked one of the buses and got on board, bound for the big HK on J. HK on J refers to the "H (Historic) K (Thousands) on J (Jones Street)"—where General Ass meets.

Let me back up.

Listeners of my radio show had wanted me to cover Moral Monday in Raleigh live at street level. And I wanted to do it. For the Asheville event in August 2013, it was easy to broadcast the show from a tent onsite, but logistics were something of an obstacle a to broadcasting live from the state capital. However, when it came down that HK on J would be on a Saturday, February 8, "my fans" (I love saying that!), including, in particular, a super guy name Mike, pushed me to get on the bus and see it for myself. Mike even arranged my seat, so all I had to do was show up.

HK on J grew into Moral Mondays under the guidance of the NC NAACP, whose members had been out there on the street, pushing for justice, since 2006. In fact, the first HK on J had been in February 2007, when Democrats controlled the entire state government. There had been one in April 2013, which led to the name Moral Monday Movement, which quickly took shape, and took hold.

It matters that the leaders and supporters of this movement had been there for over eight years, working to effect positive change, long before Puppet Pat and the far-right takeover of the 2012 election. The movement was not a partisan one, and to this day its leaders maintain its nonpartisan nature. The big difference was that in previous years the politicians had met with them and discussed their concerns with respect. After Pat and his team took over, they were greeted with locked offices, closed blinds, literally running away from their own citizens, and finally arrests for their civil disobedience in refusing to leave the General Assembly building.

There was a real buzz in the air with the 2014 HK on J, as a result of the momentum of the Moral Monday Movement and the tremendous success it had found in the hearts and minds of the people of the state of NC and beyond. Indeed, other states were already forming similar movements within their borders, and seeking the advice of Rev. Barber and the NAACP.

So on this particular morning, the buses rumbled out of Asheville by 5 a.m. and reached Raleigh some four-and-a-half hours later.

There were thousands of people gathering for the a planned march to the end of Jones Street, with the Capitol building behind the stage. People were speechifying, and others were handing out informational fliers in the swirl of excitement.

Hundreds of people from Asheville were there, mixing with others from across the state. I interviewed many of them as I walked along. I had taken some recording equipment from the station so that I could capture the event and report back on Monday. I had also gotten a prime spot up front, near the stage with the other media folks, and had called up Mikey and Mario of Asheville Channel dot com and got them press credentials as well. They had been there by my side at Mountain Moral Monday in Asheville, where we were the only people to broadcast the entire event—I on my radio show, and they on their video stream. It felt right to have them with me in Raleigh too.

What followed was almost surreal.

I made my way past the crowds that were gathering some distance down from the stage area. They were going to line up and march down at 11 a.m. I entered the area where the marchers would soon come, and it was eerily empty, as it had been closed off for the event. I walked along, thinking that it felt like something out of *The Walking Dead*. Then I reached the press area and got set up with Mikey and Mario.

A short time later, everything kicked into gear. The marchers were coming, and we could just barely hear them in the distance.

I crossed the roped-off area for the press, and, along with a number of others, moved down the street until we could see the front of the march. I took a couple of photos and stood there a moment as they got closer. And, as they did, more and more people filed in behind them.

A massive wall of people were all marching toward me, and believe me, it's a strange feeling.

I moved back to the press area and waited. The marchers grew louder in their song, and they marched right up to a few feet away from me and came to a halt, still singing.

I climbed onto the back of the Asheville Channel van and looked down the street from a slightly elevated vantage point.

I could not believe the number of people I was seeing. It was unending, as far as I could see. I looked up and saw the window and ledges of the nearby parking garage also filled with people.

As soon as the speakers began they asked folks to take a few steps forward and squeeze in, because there were still thousands of people who were at the very back who still could not get into the closed-off street area. And more were coming.

The speakers covered a variety of the topics of concern, from education, to immigration, to LGBT rights, to healthcare. The speaker for healthcare was Asheville's Leslie Boyd, whom I had gotten to know through my time on the radio, and had heard her tale of having lost her son to cancer years earlier (he lacked insurance, and couldn't afford needed treatment). Healthcare was very personal for Leslie, and she was a fighter unlike many I've known. A former reporter, she had formed Healthcare Advocates WNC, and it was her unending cause. Leslie spoke on that cool morning in Raleigh, and was, hands down, the most electrifying of the early speakers on the stage.

The main event, however, was Reverend William Barber II. And he was more than just a speaker. He was a leader, in a way that is rare to see in this day and age. He had rocked Asheville back in August of 2013, and I knew the power of his words and his presence.

It was a riveting speech. And it was faith-shaking. Especially when, near the end of his speech, he mentioned the sun coming out—and it did. For the first time, rays of sun broke through the clouds and landed right on top of the people gathered. A huge roar went up from the crowd. It was as if Rev. Barber had nature at his very command.

The rally ended, and the marchers turned and marched right back down the street, as happily and peacefully as they had arrived.

I hung back and chatted with Mikey and Mario a moment, then had to hustle to catch the bus for the ride home.

As I headed back down the street, that eerie feeling hit me again. There were very few people lingering, and it was nearly as empty as it had been on my lonely walk up. That silence was broken quickly as a booming voice called out. I ran into Russell Johnson, from Asheville, who had been there and was happily fired up by the entire event. We talked as we walked back to the bus area together.

There were still a number of folks in the bus area, but I noticed how quickly—and quietly—most of the people had already gone.

The bus ride home was filled with a celebratory vibe, and I met some great new friends, including John Spitzberg from Veterans For Peace, who shared with me the news that the International Veterans For Peace Convention was going to be hosted in Asheville in the s ummer of 2014.

A lot of talk had begun floating, trying to guess the number of people who had been there. From my vantage point, at the front, I had no way of gauging.

The next day, official numbers were released.

Somewhere between 80,000 and 100,000 people were estimated to have been there for the rally.

More than any single march in the South since Selma, Alabama in the 1960s.

Messerism #93

Moral Monday confuses Republicans by its use of the word "moral." The GOP has never understood what that word actually means.

TWENTY-FOUR
Drone, Baby, Drone

Imagine the surprise when our intrepid man on the water with his ear to the ground, Barry Summers (saveourwaterwnc.com), emailed me about his recent—and somewhat shocking—discovery about the quickly ramped-up drone industry movement in North Carolina.

Barry, who has no qualms about making politicians uncomfortable—including by attending "public" meetings that were sometimes so unpublicized that I'm sure they hoped no one from the bothersome public would know about them, let alone show up—got a whiff of something in the wind to do with drones coming to NC, and he trucked it to Raleigh to attend the meeting.

He was the only member of the public in the room.

Who was there? Well, some politicians, some drone industry types, and some members of the military and law enforcement. And Barry, who put a tape recorder on the podium, and had a humorously awkward moment later when he nearly forgot it, and had to go back and retrieve it—much to the surprise of some of the other folks who were gathered.

Barry's misadventures in Droneland

Little Timmy Moffitt (TeaBagger-Buncombe) was on the drone committee, though he had been trying to keep his constituents from knowing it. (When caught, he blamed some "mix-ups" on his official list of committees he belonged to). Of course, his major support from Tea Party types would be eroded by such news, since they most decidedly share the Rand Paul hatred of such potential invasions of privacy.

A testing location for drones was in western NC not too far from Asheville. However, not even the local government had been told that their little town was a testing site. When the mayor contacted folks in

Raleigh to express his concerns, he was basically told that he was not supposed to have found out about the testing in the first place.

Dirty water = ... Blackwater?

The whopper of the tidbits Barry brought back was the location in the eastern part of the state where a major drone-testing site was already up and running. Once he got wind of it, Barry went to Google Maps and checked it out. His discovery? Well, first, that Google Maps had not updated the label of the dubious location. And, second, that it was still labeled as the Blackwater site. Remember Blackwater? The private army thugs who were contracted at an obscenely high pay rate to "help" enforce U.S. control in Iraq about a decade back? You know, the ones who had a billion-dollar contract to do what the U.S. Marines and U.S. Army were pathetically incapable of. Yes, that Blackwater.

Amazon may be talking big talk about thirty-minutes-or-less delivery times via their commercial drones. But this series of committee meetings (all of which Barry attended) consisted of a lot of brass and law-enforcement types. I don't think they were there to talk about last-minute Christmas-shopping delivery option.

Everything old is new again

Not sure why this comes to mind, but here's a tidbit about the history of NC and armed flying capability:

On January 24, 1961, a U.S. Air Force bomber broke in half when it suffered a "failure of the right wing" (you can't make this stuff up) over eastern NC, and two nuclear bombs fell out of the B-52 and hit the ground near the city of Goldsboro. "The impact of the aircraft breakup initialized the fusing sequence for both bombs," according to newly declassified reports. Or, in layman's terms: both were armed. One landed safely after its parachute opened. The other landed in free fall. We got lucky.

And, if you want to be really scared: the Defense Department's report revealed that, between 1950 and 1980, there have been thirty-two accidents involving nukes. And there are at least twenty-one declassified accounts between 1950 and 1968, related to aircraft, in which nuclear weapons were lost, accidentally dropped, aboard planes that crashed, or jettisoned for safety reasons. Another five accidents happened while planes were taxiing or parked.

Feel better now?

Messerism # 79

I got one of those little drone-like helicopters from the guy at the kiosk in the mall. Flew it one day, and broke it. I'm a smart enough guy, mind you. I don't trust myself to safely fly one of those damned things, and I sure as hell don't trust elected officials to reasonably legislate widespread usage of more drones. Don't get me started on law-enforcement types being trusted to use them responsibly.

TWENTY-FIVE
GIDDYUP, LITTLE BRONY

You have to hand it to the folks in and around Asheville. When they make news, they make it big. Mind you, Asheville has a pretty widespread reputation for being a wildly liberal "cesspool of sin." What most people who are not from here don't realize is that once you leave the city limits, all bets are off. Typically you have to drive a number of miles to really get out to the rural fringes (I'm not knocking it—I grew up in one such place). But don't worry: you can hit a massive crop of dumbassery within five minutes of downtown if you don't hit any red lights.

In March 2014, the nation learned about a kid named Grayson in a local elementary school who had a favorite backpack from the popular children's TV show *My Little Pony*. For which he was bullied by other kids. He lived in fear of facing them, but refused to give up his backpack. One day, his mother found out that he was afraid to get out of the car because of this bullying, so she took her concerns to the principal. That brilliant lady suggested the bullying was Grayson's fault for wearing the backpack.

Yes. It was the victim's fault.

What followed was national news coverage.

Along with local dipshits who claimed that perhaps the kid who loved *My Little Pony* was the actual bully—because he refused to do what the other kids demanded—and that it was all an attempt to gain fame. That's the same logic that says that a white woman married to a Kenyan gave birth to a little mixed-race baby before desegregation and the Civil Rights movement, and decided—in 1961—that it was crucial that she fake a Hawaiian birth certificate and even insert false birth notices in Honolulu newspapers because she somehow knew that that little black baby would be running for president forty-five years later.

Of course with all the national notice, along with national and local pressure, and viral ridicule of the witless principal, the school finally welcomed Grayson back, "Pony" backpack and all.

Not one of our brightest moments, for certain.

And, of course, without it being the overt part of the whole scandal, this churned up the issue of gay rights. Because of course any boy who likes *My Little Pony* must obviously, unquestionably, revoltingly be homosexual. Everybody knows real boys like ... guns and ATVs and Republicans.

But then people started to share links to the documentary about "Bronies," who are boys who like the *My Little Pony* universe and have created an entire sub-culture within the geek world.

I found this interesting; the more I looked into it the more I realized that the whole concept of bullying over this is a 21st-century version of old-fashioned ignorance.

I recalled my love of comic books, *Star Wars*, and such things. It's a love that I still nurture. I still go to comic book conventions. I still enjoy *Star Wars* collectibles (though having a kid younger than 12 allows me to use him as an excuse for my obsession). I remember how many looks of scorn from the too-cool-for-school crowd, when I had my comics out at lunch in middle- and high school.

I also recall that in 1989, when I was a senior, all those cool kids were wearing Batman T-shirts in anticipation of the coming movie. And for the past twenty-five years, the geeks have inherited pop culture, as comic books are now among the hottest properties in film and TV.

Revenge of the nerds!

And I remember how my son, when he was three, was in love with a mini-kitchen play set that was on display in the local Target store. He would rush to it every time we went in there. And after a (very) short debate, his mother and I bought it for him for Christmas. He was beside himself with joy to have it to play with, and call it his own. As an added bonus, I got to see the slowly dissolving unease in the face of his conservative grandpa and my own rural, old-world father.

My stepson took ballet recently, and loved it. The instructors are desperate for boys to join, because there is such a stigma, and so few boys take ballet.

The whole idea of boy toys and girl toys is just insane. As is our inability as a society not to be freaked out by it.

Last year my stepdaughter got to pick out a baby doll as a reward for something or other. She rushed to the dolls and picked out a little African American baby doll, which she was overjoyed with and deemed to be "perfect." She named the baby doll "Rina," and when her mom asked why, she pointed out that the baby was dressed as a ballerina. It was that simple. She, being six, didn't see race—or at least didn't see it as anything important. She saw beyond it. Or around it. Or right through it. It just wasn't on her radar for decision-making.

We do a horrible disservice when we impose our prejudices and biases on our children. And in the more rural areas, and the places where there are uneducated people, they are letting their ignorance and fear seep into these innocent kids, who then go out of their way to bully any child who isn't tainted by the poison of such hate.

Jeff Messer

TIGHT-FITTING NATIONAL BRIEFS #6
High Times in Colorado and Washington

Man, those off-off year elections can lead to some interesting things. Colorado gets two distinctions for 2013: having five counties vote to form a new state, and legalizing recreational marijuana use. Washington State also legalized pot.

After initial shortages (supply and demand, man!) things got rolling. And it turns out it is quite profitable, and helpful to the tax base. And—I can't stress this enough—the world didn't, repeat, did NOT, come to an end!!!! No. The world still exists, and revolves on its axis, and orbits and sun, and is inhabited by paranoid insaniacs.

You can't get a man with a gun! But they can get you.

A slew of gunslinger-loving "Open Carry" laws came into effect in 2014. In fact, one town in Georgia actually made it a law that every citizen MUST own a gun. Bravo, Doc Holiday!

What followed was hordes of hicks wandering around with their guns slung over their shoulders, or holstered and poised for a quick-draw competition in the street at high noon.

These folks strutted their "rights" by turning up in some rather interesting places. We were all regaled by photos of these awfully manly folk (women included) showing off the size of their pieces while strolling up to the picnic tables at Sonic drive-ins. I guess no one told them that the food was already dead. No need to hunt it down. Then we saw folks shopping at Target with their AR-15s. I suppose the name of the store might have fooled them. Or they got lost on the way to K-Mart or Walmart.

The right-wing irony here was when the old trope of the "free market" came to bear on the over-eager Second Amendment's darned minders.

It turned out that reasonable people buying their chili-cheese tots and blue coconut slushes, and shoppers looking for diapers and toothpaste, didn't see the need for the Long Riders to be rolling up on those types of locations. And they complained. Mightily. Moms Demand Action for Gun Sense in America used all the new social media to threaten boycotts. And suddenly businesses had to choose between allowing Cletus and the Darling Gang to play badass with their guns, or, you know … making money off of paying customers who weren't being obnoxious assholes. One by one they caved to the American Way of going for the gold. Sonic. Starbucks. Chili's. Chipotle. Target.

Profits, five. Gun nuts, zero.

Messerism #107

I support the Second Amendment. I don't have any problems with responsible gun ownership. However, the gun-nuts driving the frenzy that cites the 2nd Amendment clearly have not thought it through. They obviously haven't read it, or have a reading comprehension problem. You know that part about a "well-regulated Militia?" I understand what that means. Do they? We should just start enlisting everyone who buys a gun into National Guard simultaneously, just to watch the befuddled looks on their faces.

TWENTY-SIX
FRACK YOU, YOU FRACKED-UP FRACKERS!

I love how the word "frack" has now become so casual and common place in the modern lexicon. I'm almost certain that there was as much pride as there were chuckles at the Oxford English Dictionary meeting where they discussed words that should be official additions to the English language in 2013.

Now, I'm old enough to remember it before it became the dirty word it is today. Of course, back in 1978 it was spelled "frak" and was used as a clever curse-word substitute on the Sunday night ABC TV series *Battlestar Galactica*. Even at eight, I knew that "frak" was a substitute for a dirty word (though I didn't know which one).

Galactica used the spacey term "felgercarb" as an expletive, too. And, of course, neither word's true meaning was hidden from most adults watching. But the show creators managed to dupe the ABC network censors. Go figure.

And there it was: Ol' Pa Cartwright from *Bonanza*, in a spiffy blue bathrobe, running around in space with a robot dog and Faceman from *The A-Team*, and Richard Hatch (not the first big gay winner of *Survivor*), all leading a ragtag fleet on a lonely journey to find the long-lost planet Earth! (And, if they had ever found it and seen how we humans were running things, they surely would have turned around and gone back to live with the Cylons).

Of course "frack" with the "c" in it, didn't catch on back in 1978. But it did when *Battlestar Galactica* was re-booted and modernized in 2004 on the Sci-Fi Network (before they re-branded to the incredibly lame SyFy Network some years later.) And, like a ten-year-old who just learned a new dirty word, the new show leaned into the F-word with gusto and giggly delight. They could shoe-horn a "frack" into a line of dialogue like nobody's business, though they never achieved the same level of smooth and easy finesse with which Al Swearengen could slide a casual "cocksucker" into just about any line in writer David Milch's HBO western *Deadwood*. That was pure poetry and an art form unto itself.

Now, let me stop here and admit, honestly, that I could have just as easily used the word "Hooplehead" instead of "cocksucker" and it would have been just as funny. Al (played by Ian McSchane) was a master of the profane, and sure could turn a phrase. However, "cocksucker" just has a special ring to it. And I don't think I've ever used the word before in anything I've written. Ever. This is a first. And I've just done it three times. It feels oddly liberating. Plus, we're more than 80% through this book now, and if you haven't been offended before now, honestly, there's little to no hope for you at this point.

But, here we are in 2014, where "fracking" is an even dirtier word today than Glen Larson or Ron Moore could have imagined. But where did it come from? No one should be surprised to learn that such a dirty word comes to us from such a dignified source as the mighty Haliburton.

Remember Halliburton? The no-bid, billions-in-profits, Dick-Cheney-employer that made obscene profits from the Iraq and Afghanistan wars that he started, that kept him on the payroll even when he became vice-president, then moved its operations to the United Arab Emirates in 2008 to dodge taxes on its obscene profits? Yeah. Them.

Well, they have this little mad-scientist formula of undisclosed chemicals they've come up with, which you shoot into the cracks of the earth that they drill to crack open deep pockets of shale, releasing natural gas that they then mine and sell. Sounds safe, right? And wholesome for the planet, too.

And, in case you missed it: I did say "undisclosed chemicals." Unsurprisingly—see "free market" above—Haliburton paid enough to buy up enough Congresspersons to make sure that they could keep secret the list of dangerous chemicals that they are shooting at high velocity into the ground, and potentially contaminating the planet and the ground water, as well as causing wider cracks and instability in the fractures and faults that are there, and are being created.

Safe as houses, right?

But then you ask, why would they need to hide the chemicals from the public? Makes you wonder. I could only come up with two possible reasons:

1. If We the People knew what the chemicals were, then anyone could do it. Right? Little Helen and her Christmas-gift chemistry set (do they make those any more?) could replicate the detailed formula, and she could go out in the back yard, dig a hole with her trusty pooch Rusty, fill a super-soaker with the chemicals, shoot them into the hole, and presto bazinga! Faster than you can say *Beverly Hillbillies*, little Helen and her family are fracking billionaires!

That's one possible reason.

2. The chemicals are so dangerous that people would lose their shit to know that these greedy goons are filling the ground with them, potentially setting off earthquakes, and potentially poisoning the ground water and the air. You know, those unimportant things that people drink and breathe.

As fracking has grown, so has the seismic activity around the places it has been going on. Oklahoma's waving wheat is actually shaking more now than waving, as the earthquake activity has spiked there, following widespread fracking. Of course, the folks behind it act surprised that people would even think that they had anything do with it. One huge coincidence, you know?

Because, really, there's absolutely no direct, smoking-gun proof that putting vast amounts of pressurized water and sand and chemicals a mile or two below the surface of the earth so as to crack the bedrock and release a certain kind of oil and gas could possibly case that same bedrock to crack as a result of all that added pressure. And, for sure, there's absolutely no direct, point-the-finger proof that causing the earth's bedrock to crack and move and quake causes ... you know, earthquakes. I mean, where does that silly idea come from? See, there's nothing to look at over here, folks.

What do you mean Oklahoma hasn't experienced earthquakes like this in living memory, and suddenly it had 109 in 2012, and 207 in 2013, and 241 in just the first six months of 2014? And don't forget that 5.9 magnitude quake—the largest ever recorded in Oklahoma—in

2011. Don't be silly. No connection at all. Don't look at that man behind the curtain.

But, hey, the U.S. Geological Survey suggests that it's not the actual fracking process that causes the earthquakes. It's the wastewater produced in the process. A report by Rebecca Leber in *The New Republic* magazine notes, "In fracking, a well is drilled into shale rock deep underground and a slurry of water and chemicals is forced into the rock, fracturing it and freeing up the oil or gas within. But then something must be done with the contaminated water that returns to the surface. The treated water is, disposed of in a second well—a 'wastewater injection well'—which may trigger earthquakes by pressuring and lubricating faults."

So, see, it's not the fracking at all. It's those damned, do-gooder environmentalists' fault—because if Halliburton had their way, they'd just spray the wastewater over somebody else's fields or front yards, or pour it back into the Mississippi where it would flow away and not be a problem anymore. Dirty enviros, causing earthquakes.

Thank goodness North Carolina is not a place that has plentiful oil in shale pockets, deep beneath the surface. Whew! They'll never come looking here. Right?

Wrong.

In 2014, NC got the shocking news that the Puppet Pat regime was fast-tracking fracking in our state.

Apparently three counties (of the one hundred in the state) have some smallish shale deposits beneath them. So, in the spirit of no drop left behind, of course we have to get it! Mind you, the sizes of the deposits seem so small that it wouldn't likely be cost-effective to establish fracking operations in NC and turn a profit. At least, it would seem so.

Well, at least no matter how it shakes out down east (pun intended), we're all safe and sound here in the mountains, right? I mean, there isn't anything here to find. Geological surveys over the past century have proven this to be fact, and it would clearly be a waste of time and energy to even come looking in western NC. Right?

Wrong.

In the announcement of the ham-fisted new law, we learned that seven western counties were on the list of places to be explored. Explored for what? We already know there's nothing there for them to find. And, if they can read, they know it too.

To top it off, the far-western counties named include those that are within the Great Smokey Mountains National Park. Federal lands! And one includes the Cherokee Indian Reservation.

How could they do this in those places?

No one asked, and I'm sure they had no answers.

A real head-scratcher.

What the frack is going on here?

So, let's pick this thing apart slowly and see if we can figure it all out.

My first thought, especially about the western counties, was that this was a crony payoff. The state has so little shale, and would produce such a tiny amount (if any) of natural gas, that no reasonable fracking company would be interested in investing here. So, perhaps a multi-million-dollar payoff for them to just poke around in the mountains looking for something they know isn't there could sweeten the pot. But that seems foolish.

An op-ed in *The Raleigh News & Observer* pointed out that a renowned scientist had attended many of the meetings with major fracking industry leaders. He pointed out that every time NC was mentioned, the attitude of the people in charge of fracking was that NC was not a good place to go looking, and they were incredibly dismissive. So why were the state leaders pushing it so hard?

The more I looked into it, the more it seemed like there had to be something else that we were not seeing or hearing. It just wasn't adding up. But then, I wasn't using GOP math—or logic.

Was this a distraction?

Part of the new law included a provision that sent many into a major rage, including me, initially. As part of this new law, it became a felony for anyone in North Carolina to reveal the chemicals that are used in the fracking process.

A felony.

Mind you, in 2011, the U.S. Congress released the findings of a hearing on fracking, and it included the full detailed list of chemicals. It is a simple Google search: "Fracking chemical list Congress." Or simply go to: http://democrats.energycommerce.house.gov/index.php?q=news/committee-democrats-release-new-report-detailing-hydraulic-fracturing-products.

Here were some of their findings:

- The 14 leading oil-and-gas-service companies used more than 780 million gallons of hydraulic fracturing products, not including water added at the well site. Overall, the companies used more than 2,500 hydraulic fracturing products containing 750 different chemicals and other components.
- The components used in the hydraulic fracturing products ranged from generally harmless and common substances, such as salt and citric acid, to extremely toxic substances, such as benzene and lead. Some companies even used instant coffee and walnut hulls in their fracturing fluids.
- Between 2005 and 2009, the oil-and-gas-service companies used hydraulic fracturing products containing 29 chemicals that are known or possible human carcinogens, regulated under the Safe Drinking Water Act (SDWA) for their risks to human health, or listed as hazardous air pollutants under the Clean Air Act.
- The BTEX compounds—benzene, toluene, ethylbenzene, and xylene—are SDWA contaminants and hazardous air pollutants. Benzene is also a known human carcinogen. The hydraulic fracturing companies injected 11.4 million gallons of products containing at least one BTEX chemical over the five-year period.
- Methanol, which was used in 342 hydraulic fracturing products, was the most widely used chemical between 2005 and 2009. The substance is a hazardous air pollutant and is on the candidate list for potential regulation under SDWA. Isopropyl alcohol, 2-butoxyethanol, and ethylene glycol were the other most widely used chemicals.
- Many of the hydraulic fracturing fluids contain chemical components that are listed as "proprietary" or "trade secrets."

The companies used 94 million gallons of 279 products that contained at least one chemical or component that the manufacturers deemed proprietary or a trade secret. In many instances, the oil and gas service companies were unable to identify these "proprietary" chemicals, suggesting that the companies are injecting fluids containing chemicals that they themselves cannot name.

You can read it for yourself at: http://democrats.energycommerce.house.gov/sites/default/files/documents/Hydraulic-Fracturing-Chemicals-2011-4-18.pdf.

Or just keep reading below for the list of chemicals (as released on my radio show's blog) that are used in fracking and raised some concerns:

Chemical Components of Concern: Carcinogens, SDWA-Regulated Chemicals, and Hazardous Air Pollutants:

Methanol (Methyl alcohol) HAP 342
Ethylene glycol (1,2-ethanediol) HAP 119
Diesel19 Carcinogen, SDWA, HAP 51
Naphthalene Carcinogen, HAP 44
Xylene SDWA, HAP 44
Hydrogen chloride (Hydrochloric acid) HAP 42
Toluene SDWA, HAP 29
Ethylbenzene SDWA, HAP 28
Diethanolamine (2,2-iminodiethanol) HAP 14
Formaldehyde Carcinogen, HAP 12
Sulfuric acid Carcinogen 9
Thiourea Carcinogen 9
Benzyl chloride Carcinogen, HAP 8
Cumene HAP 6
Nitrilotriacetic acid Carcinogen 6
Dimethyl formamide HAP 5
Phenol HAP 5
Benzene Carcinogen, SDWA, HAP 3
Di (2-ethylhexyl) phthalate Carcinogen, SDWA, HAP 3
Acrylamide Carcinogen, SDWA, HAP 2

Hydrogen fluoride (Hydrofluoric acid) HAP 2
Phthalic anhydride HAP 2
Acetaldehyde Carcinogen, HAP 1
Acetophenone HAP 1
Copper SDWA 1
Ethylene oxide Carcinogen, HAP 1
Lead Carcinogen, SDWA, HAP 1
Propylene oxide Carcinogen, HAP 1
p-Xylene HAP 1

So, call me a felon!

How could the radical-right regime in Raleigh hope to keep people from finding or sharing information that was widely available? Were they planning to make North Carolina more like China or North Korea, and limit the ability of all citizens to access certain parts of the Internet?

It just doesn't add up. Why make it a felony, and why deliberately make so many people so angry?

Of course, if you get slapped with a felony, you lose your voting rights. Which helps reduce voter opposition. And clearly, those who would release or share the info are not voting for them. So, that's a possibly motive. But, can you imagine the outrage? Can you imagine the major media coverage that would follow such a move?

So what then? What is going on in NC with this fracking law?

Oh, how about this little thing called Spectra Energy. Puppet Pat is heavily involved with them. He's got more than a little vested interest in Spectra Energy. Who are they? Well, for one, they have this dandy little pipeline snaking its way down the East Coast. And, lo and behold, eastern NC is a prime place for that pipeline to travel through!

OK, so there's something worthy of note there.

How about the talk and plans for opening up the coast of NC to offshore drilling? We've got a pretty large coastline.

So, the more you think about it, the more it seems like perhaps the whole fracking thing was meant to be over the top, and cause a huge uproar in response to it. It instantly became one the top protest causes in the state, which serves to distract from other things that are going on.

Mission accomplished?

Add in the semi-super-secret drone industry talks (see Chapter 24), and I believe that the entire fracking law and plans are little more than a way to keep the public angry and occupied with something that isn't as serious as we think it is. And while we're all grinding on and on against it, they're taking advantage of our distraction and pulling some other, far more important levers. It's all a smokescreen.

So, call me a felon, *and* a conspiracy theorist.

Bottom line: They won't find much here, in the way of success with fracking. But I do think they got all they wanted and more when the public embraced the anti-fracking sentiment. It allows them to use it as a diversion for something else. Something bigger. Something more sinister, perhaps.

Messerism #91

The main problem with low voter turnout isn't voter apathy, or campaign finance, or even dark money. The main problem is that, by not voting, the politicians you bitch about actually think you love them and what they are doing. They think we've got Nightingale syndrome, while we view them like James Caan's character in Misery viewed Kathy Bates.

TWENTY-SEVEN
PRIMARY FOCUS WAS SECONDARY

Something is clearly wrong when the powers that be were over the moon to learn that a little more than 15% of the local population turned out for the May 2014 primary. Mind you, we're used to about 9% turnout, and progressives were optimistic for 11% or 12% this go-round, thanks to a lot of voter remorse over the current control in the state. So I guess 15% is tremendous, all things considered. But it's one hell of a dead man's curve to be grading things on.

A total of 27,527 of 184,074 voters cast ballots.

I voted. And I hammered away on-air, and in my circle of influence, that everyone should vote. If for no other reason than to scare politicians straight. I mean, let's imagine how many of them might have wet their pants and pant suits, just a little bit, had the voter turnout have been 25%, or maybe 40% (that would have led to some spontaneous soiling, no doubt). Or imagine all of the politicians waking up to find somewhere over 50% voter turnout for a primary.

At my polling place, I got in and out within five minutes. No wait at all. And, to their credit, the poll workers were efficient and helpful. One lady even bothered to inform me (and I assume, everyone else) that, as of 2016, we would all need to have the proper and acceptable ID with us in order to vote.

"Not if we can get it right in November," I said in reply.

She stared at me blankly. I'm guessing she didn't get too many people with snappy and subtle political commentary at the ready.

For the most part, the results were predictable. NC House Speaker Thom Tillis defeated his numerous GOP rivals, and Senator Kay Hagan took 86% of the votes to easily win the Democratic nomination.

Creepy Tea Party candidate Richard Lynch lost his bid, no thanks to some pretty unsettling talk on his website, and a campaign sign that was just about the most disturbing thing of the whole primary season. The message emblazoned on this stark black-and-white sign: "Freedom or Force. You decide."

Just reading it sends shivers, doesn't it? And one can only wonder why his campaign would think that such a message would be embraced. Of course, he's also quoted on his website saying, "I would rather die fighting for what is right, then to live accepting what is wrong".

—Richard Lynch

Yes, that's exactly how it appeared on his website. Either he said, or his campaign transcribed, "then" instead of "than." Not that most of the people he was pitching to would notice. But it is ironic, right? Unless it's not a typo, and he means that he'd rather die first, and then come back to life in the world he left behind—the world full of wrong. Which, given his general logic, might be the case.

Happily for the sane world, he lost.

Sadly, so did Buncombe County Commissioner David King, a moderate Republican primaried by the Tea-Party wing of the right wing. They thought King spent too much time trying to be a moderate, and worked too closely with the five Democrats on the Commission, and tried too hard to accomplish something akin to success for the county. Which, of course, is anathema to the Tea Party. So they turned out intensively for TP-darling Miranda deBruhl, and Commissioner King lost the primary. And to the chagrin of the sane people of the county, there was no Democrat on the ballot at all.

In a surprise turn, disgruntled Republicans, appalled Democrats, and worried Independents mounted a write-in campaign to get King's wife, former teacher Nancy Waldrop, on the ballot as an independent. They garnered more signatures than the number of votes cast in the primary.

Voter Registration numbers, NC
Republicans: 1,996,272
Democrats: 2,754,825
Libertarians: 23,601
Unaffiliated: 1,743,084

REAL LIFE UPDATE #6

2014 brought many a splendid thing to my life. In addition to getting married, and writing this book, I got to host *The Norman Goldman Show* on three occasions—April 8, June 26 & 27—taking my brand of talk radio to a nationwide audience.

Also, I completed the final draft of my screenplay about the heritage of Abraham Lincoln and his connection to NC. Production is scheduled to begin in late 2014 or early 2015, with a late 2015 or early 2016 release date planned. The piece has had numerous temporary titles, including: *Nancy Hanks: The Rest of the Story*, and *Nancy Hanks and the Lincoln Enigma*. The quest continues for just the right title.

In early June 2014, I took a day trip to Knoxville to attend "Fanboy Expo." This is a great little convention of science-fiction and comic-book lovers like myself. The likes of Jonathan Frakes, Margot Kidder, Barry Bostwick, and cast members of shows like *The Walking Dead* and *Firefly* were there, but I wasn't there to see them: I had a higher purpose.

I went to see comic-book legend Mike Grell.

When I was six years old, my late (and great) grandfather, Ransom "Buddy" Russell, returned from the corner store and handed me a comic book. He had selected it at random, but it would prove to be one of the single most influential moments in my creative life.

The book? *Superboy and the Legion of Super Heroes #219*. It was a superhero team set a thousand years in the future, who had gone back in time to recruit a teen-aged Clark Kent to come join them for Sci-Fi adventures. I was mesmerized. And the book was illustrated by Mike Grell.

Then in the early 1980s, I discovered the world of independent comics. A number of top talents from the main companies (DC and Marvel) had left the big two and gone off to form creator-owned comic companies. Mike Grell was among the first to make the move. And with it, the world of comics forever changed. No longer were they just for kids. No, these new independents wrote for an older audience.

I probably was too young, at twelve, to be reading such things, but I found inspiration in this new brand of storytelling. And when I discovered that Mike Grell had a book that was part James Bond, part Pulp Fiction Detective, I had to find out more.

Back in those days, it took some searching to find out how to get hold of these books. Comic shops were few and far between. I ended up, in 1983, discovering a weekly newspaper called *The Comics Buyers Guide* at a local newsstand. And inside, I learned about all of these new comics. Some sellers even took out ads in the paper, and you could write to them for a catalogue of back issues.

The pre-digital age was rough, let me tell you.

Grell's new creator-owned book was called *Jon Sable Freelance*, and it followed a gun-for-hire adventurer haunted by his dark past and the brutal murder of his wife and children in Africa, where he had gotten caught up in the illegal ivory trade as a game warden. Sable was a former Olympic athlete who competed in Munich in 1972, and who had met his British/Kenyan wife there as she competed in gymnastics. After his family was murdered, he tracked down and brutally killed every single person who was connected—activities that ultimately got him kicked out of Africa. Naturally, in an attempt to find some relief from his grief, Sable wrote the story of his life, thinking it was the next great American novel. But no publisher would touch it, except one woman—who wanted to publish only the stories he used to make up for his children at bedtime. And so, Sable becomes the most successful children's author in America. He has to assume a pen name, too—because he realizes that his dark past would go over with his new audiences just about as well as his new kid-lit identity would go over in the hard-boiled world of mercenaries.

Not your typical comic book material, right?

I was totally enthralled by the level of realism in the story-telling. And I was so inspired that when I began writing my Great American Spy Novel series in 1984 (at age 13), Grell's work was the single most influential touchstone to me as a young writer.

I nearly met him once in 1987, but it was not to be. And many years after becoming a playwright, I found his contact info, emailed him, mentioned my love of his work, and said I'd like to try to adapt his Sable character to stage. He was intrigued, a little, but I never followed up. That was in 2003.

In 2011 he was scheduled to appear in Atlanta, GA, at the annual Dragon Con. And, as luck would have it, I was going to be in Atlanta the very day before. So I stuck around and paid my $40 admission, just to go and meet him in person. I had emailed him again, and mentioned the previous contact, nearly a decade before, and told him I would like to pick up the conversation again. I took some of my work along to give him, and prove that I was competent and serious.

Then, again, I let too much time pass while I was busy with other projects and real-life things. But when I saw he was coming to Knoxville, I decided to finally follow through—again. I emailed, and to my surprise he still remembered me (he even said he had read the Robin Hood script and liked it.)

This time around, I realized that talk was just that—talk. I needed something concrete to give him. And so, over the six weeks before Knoxville, I sat down and did a first draft script of *Sable: A Storm over Eden*.

It was a pleasure to translate the work that had, in part, inspired me as a young writer into the art form that I had chosen to follow as an adult.

The conversation was productive, and a new relationship formed with one of my heroes. And the conversation is ongoing to bring his character to stage.

Messerism # 95

The only time most people over-achieve is when they blame the president for their lousy lot in life, when they actually should aim lower. Not in life, but in blame. Most things that directly affect your life originate at the state and local level. So in many ways dissatisfied complainers should blame themselves for voting against their own interests, or not voting at all.

Messerism Bonus

Oh, the irony of the sign I saw a Tea Partier holding at the border, during the political football (soccer) that the border children have become. She was holding a sign that simply said: "America needs Jesus." I wonder if she knew that song—and if so, how funny, and sad, she was.

TWENTY-EIGHT
THE SUMMER SO FAR: NC, 2014

Rounding up 2014, as things stand by the waning days of summer 2014, there is a great deal of dread and doom and gloom. However, there is also a great deal of hope for a brighter future.

Here's a quick rundown of where things stand:
- Asheville got one step closer to world domination, when local boy Caleb Johnson won it all on *American Idol*. Another huge distinction for the great city, as we also continued to rack up slots at the tops of lists of "Friendliest," "Happiest," "Coolest" small city in polls and rankings.
- Asheville wins its lawsuit against the state for control of the water system. Timmy Moffitt shows his ignorance is saying that he is surprised that cities even have the power to sue the state over such matters. Appeal pending, and dirty politics already lurking (among Timmy's habitual two-day whiskers) in the devious possibility of an actual takeover taking place pending the final outcome of the appeal.
- In election-year politicking at its finest, state legislators, once again led by Timmy Moffitt, react swiftly to the SCOTUS ruling by passing Senate Bill 574, which asserts that "the original law was never intended to apply to groundwater contamination and this bill absolutely clarifies the original legislative intent." A parallel scenario exists in the state at Camp Lejeune, a military base. In October, a federal judge ruled that SB 574 was not valid in the Camp Lejeune case, maintaining the ten-year period of repose and dealing a blow to those who have been affected by the contamination."
- In the U.S. Congress, Senator Kay Hagan and Representative G. K. Butterfield introduce legislation that will protect the

ability of North Carolinians harmed by toxic chemicals to seek legal recourse, in reaction to the SCOTUS ruling.
- NC House Speaker Thom Tillis and Senator Hagan are in a deadlock for her Senate seat.
- Brian Turner opens up an 11-point lead against Moffitt in the race for state House seat 116.
- The Fourth Circuit U.S. Court of Appeals in Richmond overturns Virginia's ban on same-sex marriage. This ruling also rules in North Carolina, which passed a very similar Amendment One in May, 2012. Attorney General Roy Cooper quickly announced that he would no longer defend Amendment One, as the Fourth Circuit's rulings are binding on NC; gay marriages began on Oct. 10 (see pp. 67 and 215). On Oct. 13 Tillis and Phil Berger moved to intervene with yet another appeal.

Messerism #124

The way things are going, I'm seriously thinking about getting into the pitchfork-and-torch business and setting up a kiosk outside every state capital, as well as on the steps of Congress and the Supreme Court. Or at least buying stock in it. I could buy and sell the Koch Brothers after a year's profits.

Quoting Truth to Power

"When people place their hand on the Bible and swear to uphold the Constitution and then they engage in public policy that denies 500,000 people healthcare, 175,000 people unemployment, 900,000 people the Earned Income Tax Credit, they de-fund public education and push voter suppression laws ... we need to critique that in an independent way, saying, "that's not Democrat, that's not Republican; it's immoral!"
—Reverend William Barber II

TWENTY-NINE
Mountain Moral Monday II

One year after the first one came the second Mountain Moral Monday! August 4, 2014 was one of the most amazing days of my talk-radio career.

The first MMM had been an amazing success, getting a lot of people's attention and critical acclaim. So anticipation for the second one was huge.

The date was announced only three weeks in advance, as the organizers like to play things close to the vest and not tip off the opposition too far out about the events they were holding. I knew that we had to move fast. I also knew that this year stood to be even bigger and better than the 2013 rally. After all, this was a mid-term election year, and all the causes that had stirred so many to action could be affected by the outcome.

Clearly, the powers that be in the state capital were getting more than a bit worried about the impact of the Moral Monday movement.

When the General Assembly returned to Raleigh in May for the "Short Session," they swiftly passed new rules to discourage (at the least) and deter (at worst) the protesters.

In part that was because at least one judge had requested some clarification about the laws under which nearly 1,000 people had been arrested the year before. A lot of those cases had been pushed back to help lighten the heavy overload, a number of them were being dismissed, and plenty of other arrestees were demanding their day in court. By the summer of 2014, it looked fairly likely that charges would be dropped against most, if not all protesters.

So, instead of moving to make it less difficult to seek redress from the state government, General Ass made the rules even stricter, including new noise level limits that were baffling in their banality and audacity.

On the first day of 2014's Moral Monday protests, the protesters put tape over their mouths and moved, single file, through the General Assembly building in a powerfully eerie silence.

Score one: Moral Monday.

In the weeks that followed, a group of fourteen protestors camped out in the office of Speaker Tillis, refusing to leave unless he spoke with them. He did not, and around dawn, they were arrested.

Arrests were fewer this time around, as the mode of protest changed to meet the challenges. The groups were smaller and more focused as teams were assigned specific legislators to visit with questions and concerns.

What they mostly found was locked doors and closed blinds.

The Moral Monday folks had made their plans to move on to smaller protests in other cities across the state once the Short Session closed, as it was scheduled to do in late June. However, General Ass stayed in town for almost two more weeks, trying to agree on a budget between competing House and Senate versions changing teacher pay and benefits.

As had been the case the year before, the 2014 estimates of the number of protesters were all over the place, depending on where you checked come Tuesday morning. No such case was more glaring than after a Moral Monday in Winston-Salem in late June. One newspaper reported "over 1,000" protesters, while another reported "nearly 600."

Sigh.

In fact, 2014 protest numbers were smaller. In light of the upcoming elections, and the short session at which little was scheduled to be done, Dr. Barber and other NAACP leaders had deliberately focused more on voter registration activities and less on mass turnouts.

But since Asheville had been the biggest event in 2013, there was no way they would not come back to the town that boosted them the most. The heart of the movement was the push-back in Raleigh and Gen'l. Ass, but Asheville, with little doubt, was the muscle that would help win the day.

Plans were made to set up a broadcast booth for my radio show, as we did in 2013. And this time, Program Director Brian Hall wanted to up the ante for our participation.

Journalism and radio legend Bill Press loved Asheville, and he was looking for a good reason to come back to town. I had admired him for many years, and when Brian reached out Bill enthusiastically agreed to come join us for the live coverage.

I could hardly believe it. In my year and a half in radio, I had spoken with Bill on several occasions on his show, and he had called in to my show once, but I had never met him in person. I was even a caller on his show back in 2008, when actor and activist Mike Farrell (of *M*A*S*H*) was a guest. I had loved *M*A*S*H* (another major influence on me creatively) since I first saw it in reruns back in the early 1980s, and I had met Alan Alda (another life hero of mine) a few months before.

But this time, Bill Press would be right there beside me, co-anchoring the entire broadcast, starting at 3 p.m. and continuing until the event ended just before 7. Four hours of radio, with a legitimate living legend. Is it any wonder that I felt like a cross between a fanboy and a giddy schoolgirl?

We had invited listeners to my radio show to come out early and meet Bill, since our broadcast started two hours before the 5 p.m. event, and sure enough, a number of enthusiastic fans showed up early. And I have to say Bill was wonderfully gracious, both to me and to the fans. He is the embodiment of an experienced professional—as well as simply one of the nicest and most genuine people I had met in my short time in the radio business.

I knew that Bill had been around as a national media pro for a long time, and that there was little he hadn't seen, so I was curious to see his reaction to Moral Monday, and to Reverend Barber, neither of which he had witnessed fully or up close. He had interviewed Barber on his show, but had never met him in person.

As the crowds grew in size, Bill was amazed by the signs that people were carrying, and how they were almost all about hope and love. He also remarked numerous times about the overwhelmingly positive energy that the crowds brought. This was a happy protest, unlike the hate-and-fear-filled Tea Party rallies.

In the end, the crowd was a bit smaller than the previous year, but the passion was even higher. Some estimates put the crowd at over 5,000 to perhaps 6,000 by the time it was all said and done.

In true form, the media reporting of numbers was pretty inconsistent. The prize for the most dismissive storyline came from Asheville's *Citizen-Times*, which had consistently reported 2013 attendance at 6,000 (when according to other media and the Police Department, it was between 8,000 and 10,000). They had not budged from that 6,000 number throughout the previous year. But on Tuesday morning, they reported that there were only 5,000 people there for the 2014 rally, compared to the much "larger turnout of 10,000" the year before! That was the first and only time they reported 10,000 people attending the 2013 rally—as a way to make the 2014 event look like a failure by comparison. Gotta love that "liberal media" the TeaGOP has been whining about for the past few decades.

As expected, Rev. Barber delivered an electrifying speech that highlighted many of the issues on the table. But he also shared some new thoughts that were moving and enlightening.

He spoke of how the movement, which began over seven years before, had been welcomed by the previous administration in Raleigh, and the previous General Assembly, who had seemed to want to hear them out over their concerns. He spoke of how, in 2013, the newly empowered GOP ended those conversations, which helped spur the protesters into further action.

He also spoke of his own health. He's a large man who walks with a great deal of unease. I had never looked into his backstory, and just assumed that he suffered from some disability. But when he told the crowd that he had been crippled, and unable to even walk, only a few years earlier, I was taken aback. He spoke of his doctors and the people who helped him to walk again, which helped him in taking up the causes of what is morally right.

To punctuate it all, he stopped his speech for a few moments and danced a joyous jig to the roars of approval of all who were gathered.

I had seen Dr. Barber three times in total, and I was still blown away by his power, and the inspiration that in ignited.

When the speech ended, and Bill Press and I discussed it, Bill made comparisons to Martin Luther King and acknowledged that he had never, in all of his career, seen anything like what he had just witnessed.

It was amazing enough at that. However, the moment became something far beyond my wildest expectations.

Out of the corner of my eye, I could see a lot of movement near us, and it was getting closer. As we were broadcasting, I took a quick glance to see Brian Hall and a host of others coming to us, with Reverend Barber.

Moments after his speech, Bill and I found myself in a tight huddle with the man himself. We were talking over our broadcast headsets while the Reverend's support group stood close by, as numerous people rushed to get close enough to hear or snap a picture.

Sweat was dripping down Barber's forehead, but he showed no signs of fading energy. He spoke to us and answered our questions with the same fiery passion and power that he had used to energize thousands of people only moments earlier.

After a couple of minutes, he indicated that he was ready to wrap up the interview, and then proceeded to talk for another five minutes: every word we said just spurred him onward.

I looked to my left. Bill Press was there. I looked ahead, into the face of Reverend Barber, seeing the man of true greatness up close. And I could not believe that I was standing there. That I had helped to make this moment happen.

It's a moment I will never forget.

But then ...

I am not so proud of a lot of what followed.

There was a malfunction of some sort at the parking garage nearest to the Moral Monday event. Traffic was backed up, and it was taking upwards of five minutes per car to get out of the automated gate, even with the assistance of a city parking-garage employee.

Bill Press was parked there, and needed to make a flight by 8:30. He saw the snarl of traffic, and our Promotions Manager, Jeremy Powell, ended up driving Bill to the airport in the 880 The Revolution van—and believe me, that van is not a fun ride. Bill made the flight, but Jeremy had to wait for Program Director Brian Hall to get Bill's rental car out of the garage, which took a long time, then delivered to the airport, after which Jeremy and Brian had to return to get the station's other vehicle out of the garage. I got a call at a little before 9 p.m. from Brian, recounting the tale.

Then, the big story of the rally broke: City Council juggernaut Cecil Bothwell, who had been in attendance at Mountain Moral Monday, had parked—as he usually did—in that garage. As a Councilman, he also had a passcard for the garage.

Cecil used his card to aid the garage attendant in helping people get out. He swiped his card—which worked, and resolved the traffic backup—over 60 times.

Well, his act of kindness sent local right-wingers over the edge. Huge complaints were lodged that Cecil had committed some sort of heinous act of defiance, and had ripped off the county (which runs the garage) by allowing sixty-three cars to leave without paying.

The County Manager sent him a bill for over $500, demanding he pay the maximum day rate for all sixty-four card swipes under his name. Mind you, the sixty-fourth swipe was Cecil himself departing, which he plans to contest having to pay.

The good news is that locals who saw the act as a gracious one donated money to pay off the bill.

The better news is that local County Commissioner Mike Fryar was one of the GOP politicians who raised a pretty big ruckus about it, shouting the loudest about how public servants have to have integrity, and clearly Cecil had none. Within days, it came out that in 2013 this chicken fryer himeself had used a bolt-cutter to remove a barricade at another county-run parking facility—a lot near the County Health and Human Servies building. He felt that he and everyone else should be allowed to park for free on the weekends (as close as possible to several local brew pubs). Not only did he open the lot *after* being warned not to by the County Manager: he also destroyed county property (the chain across the lot entrance). GOP integrity at work.

Fryar's act was more akin to breaking and entering, and vandalism, while Cecil's actions were viewed as rather selfless.

But the right-wingers hate Cecil, and they wanted to make some hay out of it. And thus, the biggest, most enduring story out of Mountain Moral Monday part two ended up being something I dubbed: "Parking Gate Gate."

At least that was the first big story to come of it. Another reared its head a few weeks later, after the riots in Ferguson, Missouri led all Americans to become concerned with the actions and tactics of local police.

Word got out that the Asheville Police Department had been filming the crowds during Mountain Moral Monday. This was illegal, thanks to a provision that was passed in September 2013—championed by Cecil Bothwell (he gets around!)—that protects civil liberties and prohibits just such actions.

Public outcry followed. As well it should.

Messerism #142

Recent polling showed that around 60% of Americans are angry enough about what is going on in the nation to pick up a protest sign and march for or against various things. But getting those same 60% out to vote come November? No, no. That's just crazy talk.

TIGHT-FITTING NATIONAL BRIEFS #7 'ROUND AND 'ROUND THE WORLD WE GO

Putin's Soul

Russia decided to pretend not to invade while invading Crimea, and to a lesser extent Ukraine, in the spring of 2014. Only Vladimir Putin, right? The guy Dubya told us is a good guy because "I've looked into his eyes … I got a sense of his soul." Well, that was a comfort from the guy with so much insight he believed Dick Cheney had a heart. Putin is a former KGB honcho-turned-world-leader (like Dubya's daddy, GHW Bush, former director of the CIA) who can smile at you with a look that says, "So good to see you, my friend" while his actions say, "I'll fucking kill you."

Bowe Bergdahl: the one troop NOT to support

Support the troops! Leave no man behind! Unless it's a guy with ideas Fox "news" and the rest of the wrong right-wing dislikes. That guy? Well, in that case—we'll make mincemeat of him.

After President Obama negotiated a deal to release some Gitmo prisoners (bad dudes back in the day, who have been locked up since Y2K+1) in exchange for the release of Bowe Bergdahl, who had wandered away from his post in Afghanistan several years before and been captured by the Taliban. Some members of his platoon thought he deserted. Well, if he did, we should bring him home, and conduct a thorough investigation, and court-martial him, and … you know, American justice. Certainly we should reserve judgment until all the facts could be ascertained. Right?

Well, hell, no! The Republicans have got some mid-term elections to win, and a black man in the White House to smear. To hell with this soldier. He's custom-made as a tool the GOP can use to generate hate-filled rhetoric.

Obama released the most evil masterminds in a world full of

evil! Obama freed a "Terrorist Dream Team"! Obama is a terrorist sympathizer! Bergdahl is a traitor! He converted to Islam! His father wears an Osama-Obama beard!

Time—hardly liberal, but a magazine that at least used to have journalistic standards—put him on the cover with the headline, "Was He Worth It?" Asking that about an American soldier, for godssake! All that was missing was cartoon bubbles: "Ack!" "Eek!" @#Xt1^@>!

The rabid right somehow managed to overlook the fact that former junior president Dubya Bush had released many more bad guys during his tenure—in fact, according to some reports, some of those very W-released prisoners had resurfaced as part of the new terror start-up known as ISIS, ISIL, and IS. (More on that in a few paragraphs.)

The noise level eventually died down on Bergdahl, but not before his entire family were subjected to ridicule and death threats from the slack-jawed, low-IQ, low-information folk out there who joyously ran with the hate being dealt by the double-dealing devils on the right.

They didn't actually make much noise when Bergdahl was cleared by the military after a lengthy investigation. He returned to duty within a couple of months of his release.

Fox "news" could not be reached for (or bothered to) comment.

ISIS, or ISIL ... or just plain IS

You know it's going to suck when the new kids on the block in the world of terrible terror in the Middle East are so vile that even the folks running Al Qaeda denounce them as being too harsh.

This old-school, new-era group apparently was launched amid the chaos in Syria in 2013, began calling themselves the Islamic State in Iraq and Syria. OK. That pretty well pins down where they are located. And, indeed, they spent much of their early days seizing towns, cities, oil fields, banks, and dams in western and northern Iraq—which land and property grabs provided them with massive funds to fuel further efforts—up to one or two million dollars a day from some of the oil refineries they seized.

They've got the swagger too. They claim to have religious authority over all Muslims worldwide, and they self-proclaimed quasi-royal status as a Caliphate. Yes, the medieval name for the Islamic rule that followed the death of the prophet Mohammed in 632 and continued, with more or less power, until the Mongol hordes overran Baghdad in 1258. Clearly a very modern, forward-thinking group.

But not long after they gained control over a lot of territory, they started being referred to as ISIL instead of ISIS. Hmmmm.

History buffs everywhere suddenly got that queasy feeling they used to have during the mid-'80s when nobody could agree on how to spell Libyan dictator Ghaddafi/Qaddafi/Kadafi's name.

The new "L" was just dropped into the conversation with little explanation, but when it was defined, there was a collective sinking feeling. The "L" stood for "Levant," the ancient territorial name for the region that includes Syria, Lebanon, Israel, Palestine, Cyprus, Hatay, Sinai, Iraq, Turkey, and Egypt.

But after a while, even the Levant was dropped, and the terrorists became just the plain old "Islamic State." Much more to the point, and representative of the scope of their self-image and their vision: one big, fat Islamic State under their rule.

Their activities got so heinous that the U.S. began strategic air strikes in Northern Iraq, and even helped with a series of rescue missions when local civilians were trapped in the mountains and surrounded by IS forces. Saigon 1975 flashbacks.

It got so bad that Bashar Al-Assad of Syria—who two years before had been America's latest boogie-man in the mideast—was touted as a potential leader in the pushback against IS, which of course was threatening his inherited rule even more than the U.S. had when we drew a line in the sand and decided he had to be deposed. But that was 2012; in August of 2014, he invited surveillance and bombings into Syria, to help root out and destroy the roots of IS. Yes, he volunteered to let the U.S. bomb within his nation's borders.

In addition to the swift and successful land grabs, IS proved their brutality when they beheaded journalist James Foley, who had been a prisoner for two years, and then three more civilians they were holding prisoner—two Brits and another American. They posted the videos on YouTube. These guys are quite serious. And seriously brutal.

Cantor can't

Eric Cantor, the pinched-voiced, stick-up, prissy man-bitch of the House, was the number-two guy in the GOP's Washington hierarchy. He was Speaker of the House-designate in all but name, super-powerful, full of self-importance, whiny and passive-aggressive, and, most important, politically bulletproof. Until he got primaried by a Tea Party professor, and lost. So instead of becoming Speaker, Cantor got his walking papers. And, eager to cash in, he quit his House seat a month later—because the sooner he can get past that pesky prohibition against lobbying his former colleagues, the sooner he can really cash in. Not that a $1.8-million-a-year job on Wall Street is chicken feed ... except compared to what a lobbyist can take home. It's not only almost ten times his Majority Leader's salary of $193,000, it's twenty-six times (yes, 26-x) the average earnings of his former constituents.

It really is ironic—not—that those constituents felt he wasn't representing them. After all, he's a conservative Republican, and they're conservative Republicans in a conservative Republican northern Virginia district. But in addition to spending all his quality DC time on setting the stage for his next career step, he spent among the least amount of time in his home district of all Congressmen (though Patrick McHenry is in contention for that title, too). His district is a little more than an hour's drive from Washington, but to Cantor, getting there was slightly more convoluted than travelling from the North Pole to New Zealand, with a layover in Atlanta.

Maybe the best part of the story is that he pulled a Sarah Palin and quit representing those constituents for good six months before his term ended, leaving them with ... taxation without representation, which the original Tea Party folks just abhorred, remember?

Hobby Lobby and their lobby hobble

Ah, the good old, predictable U.S. Supreme Court. There was no bigger controversy in 2014 than the so-called "Hobby Lobby" case. The owners of the beads-and pipe-cleaner chain were up in arms over ObamaCare's requirement that they provide birth control coverage to their employees. These guys, the Greene family, are Christ-y to the Nth degree, and it give them the unholy heeby-jeebies to know that they are being forced to provide pills that block the assault of sperm on eggs in the way that God wants. (For years before ObamaCare, they provided that very coverage for their employees, but ... back then they weren't forced to by a Muslim Kenyan fascist communist Nazi interloper.) So they wanted the Supreme Court to give them the okey-dokey to opt out, for religious reasons. As a corporation, they wanted to be exempted from anything that challenged their corporate religious faith. In essence, they wanted to take "corporations are people" one step further to "Corporations are Christians."

And SCOTUS agreed.

Head slap!

Yes, they did. The five Catholic right-wingers—Roberts, Scalia, Thomas, Alito, and Kennedy—proclaimed the new SCOTUS Constitutional guarantees that corporations (which don't exist in the actual Constitution) can be religious people too! How about that?

Of course, smart people quickly found supporting scripture citing that, based on religious belief, all debt should be forgiven. Ooops! And the Church Of Satan stepped up and declared that they wanted the same sort of allowances for their devilish beliefs.

Pandora's box just got super-sized, and the lid blown off the hinges.

Israel goes gaga over Gaza

I know you will all be shocked, but Israel spent part of its summer vacation bombing the crap out of the folks in Gaza.

Never mind that residents of Gaza have systematically been pushed into a smaller and smaller area since the state of Israel was created in 1947.

The unrest has been a constant for as long as I can recall. Getting a settled peace in the Middle East has been a preoccupation of every leader of the United States since Richard Nixon and his Great Game tutor, Henry Kissinger. Well, maybe not Gerald Ford, who didn't have time in his year and a half in office. But Jimmy Carter, Ronald Reagan, Poppy and Junior Bush, Bill Clinton, and Barack Obama have all spent an inordinate amount of time—or their Secretary of State's time— no this fool's errand. Over the decades Israel had become less and less interested in a reasoned and rational reaction or solution; they've turned right-wing just like Washington over the past thirty years (Bibi Netanyahu even hired American political operatives to run his and the Likud's last campaign).

Of course, the Israelis have the luxury of knowing that every politician in the U.S. will go out of their way to suck up to them and their American counterpart, AIPAC; with very few exceptions, Democrats and Republicans alike support and justify whatever Israel decides to do. If Israel took live puppies from Palestinian pet shops and started roasting them in the town square of Bethlehem, the U.S. would find some way to say that it was perfectly OK. That's the way we roll. Or roll over.

Claims that Hamas (radical baddies designated a "terrorist group" by the U.S. government) were driving the car bomb of opposition were enough to justify massive missile strikes. They threw some rocks! Israel unleashed a flurry of Patriot Missiles. U.S. comment: that seems like a proportionate response.

Apparently, the folks in Gaza took exception to the glorious Warsaw-like ghetto they were generously allowed to have by the magnanimous Israel, and were looking to push back. They dug some tunnels, from which they could strike back.

Unleash the hounds of war! More missile strikes. U.S. comment: well, they clearly were asking for it.

After seven weeks of relentless strikes, a couple of coffee-and-smoke-break-long cease fires, and a lack of accountability—oh, and 71 Israelis dead, 66 of them soldiers; and 2,127 Palestinians dead, most of them civilians, at least 500 of them children—in late August a truce of sorts was reached. And, in this endless environment of violence, retribution, rinse, repeat, they actually had the audacity to announce that a "long-term" truce had been reached. I guess such things are relative. To the people involved, "long-term" could mean anything longer than a couple of days.

Border crisis

So, George W. Bush was Governor of Texas for six years, then President of the United States for eight. He was followed in Texas by GOP goober Rick Perry (who found himself indicted during the summer of 2014, diminishing—though not by much—his hopes of being the next Texas dope in the White House). Perry has been the longest-serving Texas governor ever, and, somehow, in his and Dubya's span of twenty years, the Texas border has allowed the flow of illegals like a leaky sieve.

Therefore, it clearly is Obama's fault.

The border did become a more defined crisis in during the summer of 2014, as thousands upon thousands of children ended up in massive holding areas after fleeing from Central America to the U.S. Most were sent by parents who wanted to get them away from the repressive regimes and violent drug wars there, so they could meet up with relatives in the U.S. and find better lives.

Naturally, after years of not caring about the illegal immigrants (John McCain even wrote legislation, based on Saint Reagan's identical program, promoting quasi-amnesty), the right wing lost their collective mind over the sight of little brown kids coming here, trying to flee oppression. Amnesty? Fuggedaboudit.

Tea Partiers were first off the mark, during the 2008 campaign, when John McCain asserted he "wouldn't vote for [his own legislation] at this point." In 2012, Mitt Romney demanded they "self-deport." But by 2014, the whole Republican Party, self-styled "moderates" as well as the GOP's vast right-wing majority, had a new solution for those kids: arrest them, incarcerate them, and send them back to the Ecuadorean death squads whence they came. Because it's only pre-born children who deserve the right to life, and these aren't pre-born anymore, so who gives a ... whatever.

Besides, according to the leading lights of the TeaGOP, they're probably A) drug-runners with "calves the size of cantaloupes because they've been hauling seventy-five pounds of marijuana across the desert" (Steve King, R-IA); B) Islamic "terror-babies" (Louis Gohmert, R-TX); or C) ebola-carriers or potential traitors (Rep. Todd Rokita, R-IN). Or, in the "minds" of Michelle Bachman, Sarah Palin, and others, junior Liberian-Nigerian-Kenyan-Muslim bio-terrorist anchor babies. Just like our illegitimate president.

I don't know, maybe we could propagate them for Soylent Green.

Jeff Messer

Messerism bonus

I was thinking of that Sunday-school children's song "Jesus Loves the Little Children." How could the same people who grew up with that song be so mean and cruel to the immigrant children on the border. Then I realized something: "Jesus loves the little children. All the children of the world. Red and yellow, black and white. They are precious in his sight...."

Wait! What! No mention of Brown. Of course!

Boehner's suit against Obama

Tired of not getting your way? Sue!

Speaker Boehner has clearly run out of tactics. Perhaps inspired by the success rate of bat-shit-crazy rulings coming out of the Supreme Court, the Speaker decided that his last tactic before the midterms would be to sue the president for overuse of executive power. Now, the last president to issue fewer Executive Orders per term than President Obama was Grover Cleveland, who was in office from 1885-89 and again from 1893-97. George Bush the first—who only had a single term—issued 168; St. Ronald of Reagan, in two terms, 381; Bill Clinton, 364, Dubya 291, and Obama, 147 in his first term and 41 more as of Sept. 20, 2014. But after all, Obama underusing his broad executive powers, as the chief executive of the nation, was just a step too far, down the path to fascism! Because ... Benghazi? Kenyan? Islamic terrorism? Presiding while black?

But, simultaneously and with true Boehnerian logic (remember, he grew up in his father's saloon), the lawsuit challenging Obama for doing too much with Executive Orders would be also accuse him of ... not doing enough. Well, at least when it comes to implementing certain portions of the Affordable Care Act.

Wait. What?

Yes. John Boehner sued Obama for not implementing parts of the ACA quickly enough. This, despite his endless objections to the ACA, and the more than fifty votes in the House to overturn it. Despite his having allowed a massive government shutdown in October of 2013 in a misguided attempt to stop the entire ACA from taking effect at all, he's now suing because Obama didn't let part of it take effect quickly enough. This is the WTF GOP logic gap in full motion. Yet the American people fall for this shit. Endlessly.

In the world of modern U.S. politics, this story would not be complete without one last word from Speaker Boehner. As his Congress left for vacation on his say-so (the Speaker sets the schedule), having refused to take any action to resolve the "illegal immigrant border crisis" (for fear of having to answer for it, one way or the other, ahead of the midterms), Mr. Boehner asserted, as he headed out for a beer at his favorite Ohio bar, that President Obama had the ability, the legal right, and the presidential prerogative, to use his executive powers to fix the immigration problem on his own.

You have to wonder if alcohol, nicotine, and orange spray-on suntan lotion combine to create a toxic stew that dissolves brain cells.

(NB: By October, 2014, the first two law firms Boehner tried to hire for his lawsuit had declined to take the case. In November, a week before Thanksgiving and the day after Obama issued an Executive Order to fix the immigration problem on his own, Jonathan Turley, a commentator for Fox, agreed to represent the Representative.)

Congress vacation daze

The best thing Congress did all year was go on vacation: we're all safer and better off with them NOT at work. Mind you, they work less than 150 days each year (in a long year). In 2014, they scheduled the shortest work calendar of any Congress ever. At least when they aren't there, they can't screw things up.

Here's some blood-pressure-raising food for thought: Congress works fewer than half the days of the average worker in America, and they are paid $174,000 per year, with a full benefits package. Now, consider the minimum-wage worker who is working more than twice as many days as Congress and making $15,000 for it. Worker at McDonald's: $15,000, 300 days, fifty bucks a day. Idler in McCongress: $174,000, 150 days, 1,160 bucks a day—plus support staff, travel allowances, subsidized meals, gym, private subways, healthcare, fully vested taxpayer-paid retirement plan, endless opportunities for spouses to cash in....

Angry yet?
Angry enough to actually vote?

Of Walgreens and Burger Kings

Summer 2014 was a great time to try and sneak out of the country in an attempt to dodge taxes and screw over the American people. Companies do this by "inversion," where they change their incorporation to an overseas location—Ireland is popular—where they can claim all their income but not have to pay taxes on it.

Walgreens tried to do it when they thought nobody was paying attention. But word got out about their plan to stick it to the American tax system, and people in Dixon, IL, raised some hell, including by channeling the name of very civic-minded company founder Charles Walgreen. Social media lit afire with memes calling them out, which reached fever pitch in a surprisingly short amount of time, prompting Walgreens to do some quick math and realize that they stood to lose more from people boycotting them than they might have gained by going off-shore. They changed their minds.

Less than a month later, Burger King surprised folks with the news of a merger with Canada's Tim Hortons (coffee and doughnut king of the Canucks). People who know Tim Hortons were salivating at the thought of getting some north-of-the-border goodness down here. But the salivation turned to raging spit when it became clear that Burger King planned to move its headquarters out of America, in another attempt to dodge taxes. And faster than you can say "Whopper," the same social-media backlash kicked into overdrive. Oddly, the BK plan wouldn't have made that big a difference tax-wise, since franchise owners are the ones responsible for most of each store's federal, state, and local taxes and they wouldn't have benefited by the parent company's inversion. BK hasn't dropped its plan, but it's said to be reconsidering.

Personally, I hope that this level of shaming catches on and becomes the new norm. Perhaps people have finally figured out how to use social media as a major weapon. That certainly helps explain the intense, ongoing attempts to stifle Net neutrality.

Holding corporations accountable is supremely patriotic. And I hope that this is just the beginning.

Another type of accountability got a major workout in the summer of 2014, as police tactics and the militarized levels to which police forces have grown hit center stage.

Ground Zero for the militarized police state

Remember the major takeaway from the post-Boston Marathon bombing: the quick, militarized response that we all saw in Boston? It was for a good cause, so we all sort of gave them a pass on it. No one really gave much thought to the larger implication of the rapid response, and how heavily armored it was.

It was only a matter of time before the other jack-boot fell. And fall it did, upon Ferguson, Missouri, in early August of 2014, when citizens took to the streets in a massive protest to the police shooting of an eighteen-year-old African American named Michael Brown.

The protests were met with a heavily armed response from local law enforcement, revealing grenade launchers, body armor, armored vehicles, and brutal tactics that made this middle-America town look like the Middle East.

The events were set off when, on Saturday August 9, Michael Brown was killed by Officer Darrin Wilson, just after noon, and in front of a lot of onlookers. His body was left in the street for hours, and the community began to question what was going on, and what the police were doing. Soon questions about the shooting, and the events that led to it, began to circulate. Brown was unarmed, and had his hands up, when Officer Wilson shot and killed him. The entire event seemed to be prompted by Brown and a friend walking in the middle of the street. There may have been a scuffle through the open window of the officer's SUV, at the end of which Brown tried to flee, and Wilson got out of the vehicle and opened fire. Within hours, word had spread, and crowds assembled to demand satisfaction.

While some details are still at issue, there were a lot of concerns over what had happened, and why, and how. And the Ferguson police seemed to be trying to spin the narrative. Instead of responding to the calls for some sort of explanation, they suited up with military-grade gear and moved in on the protestors.

What followed was a week of chaos. The police were ham-fisted in their reaction, and neither side was willing to step back. It boiled at high heat for days, and finally boiled over, when the police began to act outside the law and fire tear gas into the crowds. They roughed up several journalists, a sure-fire way to get to the top of the front page. The reaction to this massive law enforcement overreach was to descend upon Ferguson in a media circus that would put Ringling Brothers to shame.

With all eyes turned to Ferguson, the story went from a local dust-up to a national discussion. Most people wanted to know if what we were seeing in Ferguson could happen in their own towns. Where did all this military gear come from? Do all local police forces have such stuff?

Ferguson Police Chief Tom Jackson could not seem to figure out how to settle the relentless violence or answer the media's questions. Scrutiny was intense, so on August 14 the governor sent in State Police Captain Ron Johnson, an African American and a native of Ferguson. He took to the streets, unarmed and un-armored, and talked with the people about their concerns. Peace at last.

It did not last.

One of the public's major concerns—what had fueled the crowd's rage for days—was that the Ferguson police were hiding the identity of the shooter, and trying to conceal information about the shooting.

Then the radical group Anonymous released the name and a photo of Officer Wilson, and in a press conference that was the height of incompetence and awkwardness, and which blind-sided Captain Johnson, the chief tried to dispute his identity.

But Jackson's Friday press conference revealed that the police had video footage of Michael Brown appearing to steal some cigars from a local convenience store, and very quickly the peace was lost again. Jackson's implication was that Brown's theft of the cigars somehow meant that it was okay for Wilson to have shot and killed him.

It didn't help that Chief Jackson, only hours later, had to walk back the convenience store shoplifting scenario, when he admitted that Officer Wilson was unaware of the incident at the convenience store at the time of his encounter with Brown.

Oops.

So the video footage was floated out as a red herring to try to blame the victim. Fox "news" had a field day. And, to support their brand of made-up news, Fox trotted out a story that Brown had attacked Officer Wilson through the window of his SUV. (Eyewitnesses had said that Wilson had grabbed Brown through the window and pulled him into the vehicle, prompting the scuffle).

Right-wing sources published X-rays of a severe eye-socket fracture and claimed it was Officer Wilson's face; CNN later reported that the Fox report was false. Which raises the question: if Officer Wilson was squeaky clean in his actions, why would anyone need to make things up to garner sympathy for him and make Brown look like a thug?

By nightfall of August 15, Ferguson was a city under siege—again.

President Obama weighed in. Attorney General Eric Holder flew to Ferguson. The state National Guard was sent in.

As badly as the Ferguson Police had managed to mismanage the crisis, calm finally came in the second week of the chaos, thanks to the national attention and Attorney General Holder's calming presence.

Previously confiscated video and audio eventually made its way to the media, after eyewitnesses had given accounts of what happened, filmed it with their phones, then been strong-armed by the police, who confiscated the footage. Need to hide something until a cover story is fully concocted?

A Grand Jury investigation was set in motion, and the sense that some level of justice was at least in the offing finally settled things down, and the protests slowly wound down after over two weeks of unrest.

All eyes had been on Ferguson, and they now turned to their own local law enforcement agencies with some very serious questions.

What we saw in Boston in 2013 and Ferguson in 2014 were not exceptions, but the new norm. Thanks to a big Pentagon fire-sale on old Cold War surpluses under the "1033 program" back in the mid-1990s—part of the "peace dividend" from the end of the Cold War—and a newly ramped-up Homeland Security initiative in the mid-2000s, nearly every local law enforcement agency in America had gotten their hands on some pretty bitching cool gear.

Thanks to reporting locally from journalist David Forbes of *The Asheville Blade*, we learned about the inventory of our local police. *The New York Times* ran an interactive county-by-county map of the U.S. that showed a list of each county's full inventory.

Asheville and Buncombe County? Two grenade launchers, two armored vehicles, eighty-four assault rifles, to name a few. Mind you, we don't come close to some NC counties. Orange County gets the title as the most militarized in the state, but my attention was drawn to Cherokee, the westernmost county in the state, with four military helicopters, and a pair of Mine Resistant Armored Vehicles (MRAVs). Because you need that out there in the mountains.

For all the horror of watching the situation in Ferguson unfold, it served to draw the nation's attention to the militarization of the police that had been taking place. Now, We the People are pretty worked up, and police nationwide are feeling the pressure of being under a tightly focused microscope. This can only be a good thing.

Thanks to social media, much of what happened in Ferguson was captured and uploaded instantly, giving the world a raw and unfiltered view. The media didn't have time to spin it (though Fox gave it the old college try), and had to run with the story as it unfolded, unable to twist it to fit an agenda. It was happening so quickly, and so uncontrollably live. It was refreshing.

It was also quite funny to see CNN and MSNBC both run photos from the streets of Ferguson that were so much in the public eye that they could not edit or manipulate them. My personal favorite showed a line of armored officers moving toward a man whose back was to the camera with his hands up. In front of the police was a U.S. Postal Service mailbox with the words "Fuck the Police" spray-painted on the side. And both CNN and MSNBC ran the image, either knowingly or oblivious to the "F-bomb" appearing prominently on their screens.

That's real, that's radical journalism! And that's what we've been sorely lacking for a long, long time.

Democracy at stake

The hope that existed in my once-great state on that November evening in 2008 had quickly eroded. Two years later, the Tea Party influence had taken hold, and the apathy of smart, progressive voters allowed it to win. In 2012, the deal was completed with the passing of Amendment One, followed by the election of Pat McCrory as governor, allowing an unimpedable far-right-fueled rule in the state.

Now we are in a fight for our rights, as well as life.

I fear that the plan—on some level—is to make sure that those who cannot afford representation are slowly and systematically removed from the system by those in power. I suspect North Carolina is the incubator for what is yet to come in other states, should the radical far-right agenda be allowed to grow and thrive.

If they can hurt the general population in such severe ways as to cut them off from the ballot box, there will be no challenge against the draconian rule they've put in motion.

Forcing the unemployed to go without benefits drives them to take any (or many) low-paying jobs. A person desperate enough to work every hour he can just to survive cannot take the time to pay attention to politics; either from sheer exhaustion or, sometimes, from bosses who don't want engaged employees. Some workers are not given any time off from work to vote, and if they are allowed time off, they can't afford the lost wages.

Decreasing access and opportunity to vote is designed to make it harder for those who struggle to participate in the democratic process, and much easier to opt out. Low voter turnout keeps bad guys in power.

So that takes care of the working poor (who are disproportionately black and Hispanic and tend disproportionately to vote Democratic). As for the poor-but-upwardly mobile ... well, think "feudalism."

De-fund and damage public education to such a degree that only those with the affluence to send their kids to private schools will see them succeed ... along with those whose creed makes Jesus the privatizer-in-chief and are therefore eager to apply for "opportunity scholarships"—read Christian-school vouchers—to give their kids a leg up.

So much for—in Jesus-speak—the least among us.

Who else? De-humanize members of the LGBT community.

How about the elderly?

Simple: cut off Medicaid, privatize Social Security and Medicare.

Hammer wedges between "us"—upper-middle-class, hanging-on-the-edge, hoping-for-a-break, used-to-be-better, rural, ignorant, fearful, God-fearin', Jesus-lovin', "traditional," and above all, white—and all the "thems" of different races, cultures, nations, languages, faiths, sexual orientations, and above all, different ideas.

To anyone who bothers to look, it's all there, in plain view.

A lower-income, chronically unhealthy, overworked and underpaid society benefits only those of higher income, who can afford to be healthy, wealthy, and wise—and generous in buying a government that works exclusively for them.

Welcome to North Carolina under the first fully-GOP controlled capital in over a century. Now, watch as they take us all the way back to where they left off in 1896.

Or, watch us rise up and turn back the ugly red tide that is trying to wash over the Old North State.

Messerism #82

The only reason to take the high road in the world of politics in this day and age is because the high road is the best vantage point from which to throw rocks.

THIRTY
The Long Road Ahead

As the summer of 2014 came rolling toward a close, things didn't get much better. Finally, General Ass settled matters and went home to try to keep their seats, yet again leaving behind a bloody wake.

The NC budget was finally passed, and some pretty dastardly things got slipped in with it. The governor decided to sign it first and read it later.

Now, thanks in no small part to Asheville whomping the state in the lawsuit to keep our water, a new three-judge panel was put into place in NC. This trio would now be the first stop in any and all cases brought against the state in matters of challenging the legislature. Clearly, the folks in charge did not want to take the chance of losing another challenge. So why not create a new set of rules, and appoint your own activist judges who are sympathetic to the far-right agenda? That'll teach them!

And as for criminal doings by Puppet Pat, or any of his minions, cohorts, and cronies? Well, another thing Gen'l. Ass did was move the State Bureau of Investigation from the Attorney General's office—where it had been since its founding—to the direct control of the Governor's Office of Public Safety. Becase after all, the people elected Democrat Roy Cooper Attorney General, so he's not part of the governor's "team," and this way the very folks charged with investigating wrong-doing by public officials are now under the purview of ... public officials. Convenient, eh?

A sneaky part of the new budget also included the cut-and-pasted drone bill which thus became law without any public notice. Look! Up in the sky! Whoops! No, look over there. Just not behind the curtain.

Numerous groups—the NAACP, League of Women Voters, and others—sought a stay to the GOP's voting law changes until their lawsuit is heard in 2015; that way existing law would govern the November mid-term election. The stay was denied, allowing for the shortened early-voting period and keeping the voter ID laws on track for 2016; then the Court of Appeals reversed that ruling in part, imposing a stay on the prohibition against counting ballots that are inadvertently cast in the wrong precinct, and ending same-day registration and voting. The rest of the law's provisions were allowed to stand. Immediately the Legislature appealed to the Supreme Court, which, sadly, upheld the disruptive new rules so as not to "disrupt" the elections process.

Duke Energy makes little to no progress on cleaning up the Dan River coal-ash spill, despite posting $609 million in profits on $5.9 billion in revenue in the first two quarters of the year. In August the state Department of the Environment and Natural Resources (DENR) ignored the law and its own rules for water quality and sent a letter to Duke that would allow the company to empty its coal-ash ponds into rivers and streams without any testing. A DENR spokesman said the agency was following an August 1 executive order from the governor to move ahead with the closure of the ash ponds. In September the U.S. EPA overruled the state under the Clean Water Act, saying the plan would likely violate federal water quality standards. A few days later, DENR revoked its previous approval of Duke's plans.

The legislature also passed a law creating a new state commission to oversee the closure of the ash ponds. The governor pitched a hissy fit and threatened to sue, because the legislation directs that the House and Senate appoint a majority of the nine commission members; Pat the Brat got his panties in a twist claiming that since it will be an executive branch function, he should control the commission by appointing a majority. And, sure enough, the day before Speaker Boehner sued the President of the United States, the Governor of North Carolina sued the Speaker of the State House. Oh, those squabbling Republicans.

Small-town Sylva, NC, in Jackson County, voted in a ban on fracking. Since the fracking law in the state prohibits counties, cities, and towns from initiating such a ban, thereby choosing their own destiny, the town's action amounts to nothing more than a symbolic gesture. At the very least, though, it's a gesture that cities and towns throughout the state should also do, in an act of defiance. It would speak volumes.

Those fracking frackers

From late August through mid-September, a series of forums on fracking were scheduled for Cullowhee at Western Carolina University. They were hosted by the NC Mining and Energy Commission.

Tate MacQueen attended the forums, and asked me to forward my list of fracking chemicals so that he could share them at the forum, and of course subject himself to felony charges for doing so.

The last forum took place after the announcement that plans for exploration for fracking in seven western counties was no longer on the table. (It was beginning to seem that my conspiracy feeling [see p. 179] was all but confirmed. They were never coming here. There's nothing here for them to explore or find.)

The final forum was attended by more than 500 people, despite the news that fracking was no longer coming to western NC. Tate was among them. As at all the other meetings, the overwhelming public opinion was against fracking, but this time, there were also a number of men wearing pro-fracking shirts and hats.

Tate told me he witnessed one of these guys stand up and take his shirt off once he saw what was going on. The man was heard saying: "I can't believe I sold out for a sandwich."

Turns out the petroleum industry folk had brought a bus full of men from a homeless shelter in Winston-Salem, gave them lunch, and promised them jobs if they came along on the four-hour bus ride and wore the shirts and hats embossed with sayings like, "Shale Yes!"

A few days after I covered the story on 880 The Revolution, it made it onto *Real Time With Bill Maher* on HBO.

One last disclaimer: even though the pro-frackers said they'd decided not to explore WNC for shale oil and gas, freedom to frack is still state law, and they could change their minds at any time.

Amendment Minus-One: they all lived *fabulously* ever after

SCOTUS accomplished something amazing by doing absolutely nothing on October 6, 2014. The Court refused to hear arguments to overturn rulings from appeals courts in Virginia, Indiana, Wisconsin,

Utah, and Oklahoma that declared bans on same-sex marriage unconstitutional. Those rulings bind all the states under those courts, so in eleven states, including North Carolina, same-sex marriage bans were no longer allowed. By doing nothing, the Supremes increased the number of marriage-equality states to thirty.

The media were caught off guard, and stammering reporters and experts tried to process what it meant while LGBT communities celebrated around the nation. And here in Asheville, on Thursday, October 9, City Council unanimously approved hanging a huge Gay Pride rainbow flag on the side of City Hall. A photo taken by Asheville Mayor Esther Manheimer appeared on Facebook.

Right-wingers went nuts, yelling to put Jesus stuff up, too. Former Asheville Councilman and GOP political fanatic Carl Mumpower Photoshopped a picture of a Nazi flag hanging there instead. Being borderline insane, he insisted the two movements were just alike in their opression of dissent, or some such nonsense. And of course he got his desired result: national headlines before the weekend.

Register of Deeds Drew Reisinger had already made plans to keep his office open late to accommodate couples who wanted marriage licenses (see p. 69), and at a little past 5 p.m., word came that Judge Max O. Cogburn had signed an order directing state Registers of Deeds to immediately issue marriage licenses to same-sex couples. He wrote, "North Carolina's laws prohibiting same-sex marriage are unconstitutional as a matter of law. The issue before this court is neither a political issue nor a moral issue. It is a legal issue."

By 5:30 that afternoon, marriages were being performed on the sidewalk right outside the Courthouse, as excited couples came out holding their fully-legal paperwork.

Thom Tillis and Phil Berger had begged for more time to make their arguments against the rulings by Cogburn, U.S. District Judge William Osteen in Greensboro, the Fourth Circuit Court of Appeals in Richmond, and the Supreme Court. They were given until 3 p.m. on Monday, October 13 to get their hate-filled shit together. They had hired a $400-an-hour lawyer from California to fight against the changing tide.

But as I—and many others—have pointed out many times, it's hard to put a genie back into a bottle, to undo something, politically or legally, that is already done. Tillis and Berger face an uphill climb, one that will serve only to show their narrow views and their agendas of hate.

As the mid-term election approached, good news was beginning to shine through the clouds of the GOP control of the past years. Some things even their backward views and almost-absolute power cannot stop. Of course it was clear that the backlash to the unbroken string of judicial decisions at every level might motivate the right wing to get out and vote, and that could hurt candidates like Kay Hagan, Tate MacQueen, Brian Turner, and others.

Still, I have rarely been prouder of my city than in that October week when a major step forward in equality came to town, and a lot of good people stepped right up to the plate—and hit it out of the park. (The events tested many, and revealed the true ugliness of some, but not by any stretch a majority.)

I think when City Council took the brave step of hanging the rainbow flag, while the city still awaited some indication of where things would go next, they metaphorically planted the Asheville flag of love, peace, understanding, acceptance, and progress. What a wonderful commentary on their character.

Damn, I love this place.

Messerism #101

A recent meme shows a picture of Hillary Clinton with the words, "November 4, 2016: The day that racism becomes sexism." To which I say: "Vagina: the new black."

THIRTY-ONE
Electile Dysfunction

Despite the state's diminished Early Voting period, early-voter numbers were well above expectations as Nov. 4 drew closer. Compared to 2010, turnout was up in all demographics, with Democratic voters' numbers up 124% over 2010, and the GOP up 103%. Clearly voter interest was high. Then came lots of little news items about hiccups in the systems, both far and near.

In Georgia, 40,000 out of nearly 90,000 new voter registration forms that had been collected in March and April mysteriously disappeared just before election time—and, not so shockingly, just after the deadline to register. The new registrations were from predominantly black and poor areas of several major counties.

In North Carolina, there were reports that a number of Diebold voting machines—especially in Hagan stronghold Guilford County—were changing Kay Hagan votes to Thom Tillis votes after voters had finished their ballots and were about to submit them. Diebold, you might remember, is the voting-machine company whose CEO, Walden O'Dell, announced in 2003 that, as a chief fund-raiser for George W. Bush, he was "committed to helping Ohio deliver its electoral votes to the president." By 2008, numerous investigations in at least six states showed how easily the machines could be hacked without a trace to steal elections. O'Dell resigned in 2005 while the company was under investigation for securities fraud. Maybe the new owners and managers think nobody will notice if they return to their old tricks.

Meanwhile thousands of voter registrations that had been made through the NC DMV had "not been submitted properly" (or at all, or some other random "Oops: my bad!" excuse); as in Georgia, the "discovery" came too late for those people to register (again).

All major media outlets maintained the party line that the elections were a horse-race that would go down to the wire. Of course, election night is always a ratings bonanza—and cash cow—for TV and radio: $1 of every $3 spent in advertising in the fall of 2014 was for political ads, so even a walk-away win is presented by most media as a nail-biting, down-to-the-wire contest.

National results come in

The word that Mitch McConnell easily won re-election in Kentucky, as did Lindsey "Belle" Graham in SC, set a pretty bleak tone during the early-evening announcements on November 4. The Red Team were on the board early.

The ham-fisted, union-busting, Koch-sniffing Wisconsin governor, Scott Walker, won re-election in a common-sense head-scratcher, while castrating insaniac Jodi Ernst beat Congressman Bruce Braley to flip Iowa's open Senate seat (Democrat Tom Harkin having retired after thirty years). Ernst's election means the U.S. Senate will have a ready replacement for the House's unlamented, departing Tea-maniac Michelle Bachmann.

In Kansas, voters are so conditioned to vote Republican—despite empirical evidence that undiluted Reaganomics has brought their state to its economic knees—that they knelt down and gave true believer Sam Brownback another four years to wreak havoc as governor, and returned Pat Roberts to the Senate despite the fact that, like Alice, he doesn't live there anymore ... and no longer even speaks Kansan.

Florida voters, vast numbers of whom rely on Medicare, reelected as governor the right-wing, unindicted Medicare fraudster Rick Scott. His company, Columbia/HCA Healthcare, billed hundreds of millions in false claims, and, when caught, paid over $2 billion in fines and penalties. Scott resigned as chairman soon after the investigation began—and walked away without prison time, but with a $350 million golden parachute. Maybe all that Florida sun causes voter dementia.

Here at home, sadly, Thom Tillis, with his glassy, empty eyes and the creepy vacant smile of a ventriloquist's dummy (I think ALEC has its hand in the usual place, manipulating him like a satanic Willie Talk) squeaked into higher office, and sent Kay Hagan home regretting that she'd spent so much campaign time pretending not to know Obama.

With the defeat of Democrats Mark Udall in Colorado and David Pryor in Arkansas, along with Republican pickups of open seats, the GOP will control the Senate for the last two years of Obama's presidency. While the rest of the world shakes its collective head, new Majority Leader Mitch McConnell will join House Speaker John Boehner in "governing" the country ... by doing their best to stall the economic recovery and thus prove the Democrats can't govern, and thus improve the chance of Republican taking back "their" White House in 2016. I guess we've all just been more uppity than they can tolerate.

Closer to home

In U.S. House District 10, my friend Tate MacQueen lost to smug, sleazy, Patrick McHenry. (Google him. Please. As soon as you type "Patrick McH" it autofills to "enry murder," followed quickly by "gay scandal.") Tate carried Buncombe County nearly 2 to 1, but western districts were designed to eliminate Buncombe County and Asheville as a threat to GOP hegemony. So, naturally ...

... in U.S. House District 11, shutdown clown Mark Meadows decisively beat the weak, Republican-lite Democrat Tom Hill.

State House

On the plus side, Buncombe County demonstrated just why it's such a threat to GOP hegemony. First, Susan Fisher ran unopposed in District 114 for another term representing a big chunk of the county. Then Democratic farmer John Ager, son-in-law of the late Congressman James McClure Clarke, beat Republican farmer and one-term-wonder Nathan Ramsey to win NC House seat 115.

And to the joy of every lover of liberty, democracy, honesty, and good government—to say nothing of Truth, Justice, and the American Way— Brian Turner handily vanquished this book's chief villain, Tim Moffitt, in the 116th District. As the final results came in, Tim's famous five-o'clock shadow quickly darkened to midnight. Well, Little Timmy can now go to work holding out the change purse for ALEC—and since he hates Asheville so much, we're hoping he'll leave it far, far behind. I suspect he'll be flooded with offers to help him pack.

My hometown homeboy Joe Sam Queen retook House District 119 seat from GOPpy Mike Clampitt (yes, those are their real names, and no, jokes aren't allowed), representing rural Haywood, Jackson, and Swain counties. But loony, not-too-bright Michele Presnell held the 118th State House seat against Democratic challenger, and far superior candidate, Dean Hicks. Voters of Burnsville, you got some 'splainin' to do.

Farther east, laughingstock Renée Ellmers beat back *American Idol*'s Clay Aiken, so we'll have her displaying her unhinged views and embarrassing the Tar Heel State for years to come. Her hyper-gerrymandered District 2 includes parts of Wake County, so she can feel right at home among the J Street crazies in Raleigh.

State Senate

In local NC Senate District 49, Terry Van Duyn easily held off GOP rabble-rouser Mark Crawford. But our next-door neighbors in Henderson County ("all red, all the time") reelected Tom Apodaca to the District 48 seat, beating valiant tilter-against-windmills Rick Wood. Apodaca chairs the Senate Rules Committee, where he bottles up all progressive, useful legislation before it can hit the floor. For some reason, he became a hero to some environmentalists for championing tighter rules against coal slurry ponds—but somehow the tighter rules never got passed by the rest of his GOP colleagues. So he lives to ruin another day.

RUMOR ALERT: Tom Apodaca will resign for "health" reasons early in 2015; the Republican Party will appoint Tim Moffitt to fill his seat for the remainder of his term. Remember, you read it here first!

Local races

Buncombe County Commissioner Ellen Frost again out-polled self-proclaimed "Hispanic" Republican Christina "Never-give-up-my-lawsuits" Merrill—this time by far more votes than the eighteen disputed ones that gave her victory in 2012. But Tea Party darlin' Miranda DeBruhl defeated unaffiliated Nancy Waldrop, so the County

Commission still has its 4-3 Democratic majority. Only Ms. DeBruhl will never work with her Democratic ~~colleagues~~ (whoops!) enemies.

All in all, there were a lot of victories for folks here in WNC, who pushed back strongly enough against the GOP aggression from Raleigh to slay a few pretty grand dragons* like Tim Moffitt and Nathan Ramsey. The Patrick McHenry win is a bitter pill to swallow, showing the sad reality of the gerrymandered districts that require more than three Democrat votes to every Republican one to send someone to Washington or Raleigh.

Before the dust had fully risen, let alone begun to clear or settle, the media talking heads started licking their chops and chanting the magic mantra "2016." Congress stays in GOP hands, the Senate will be mired even deeper in the mud of obstruction, and Obama will have to choose whether to go out in a whimper or, perhaps, tap his inner Ezekiel 25:17:

> The path of the righteous man is beset on all sides by the iniquities of the selfish and the tyranny of evil men. Blessed is he who, in the name of charity and good will, shepherds the weak through the valley of darkness, for he is truly his brother's keeper and the finder of lost children. And I will strike down upon thee with great vengeance and furious anger those who attempt to poison and destroy my brothers. And you will know my name is the Lord when I lay my vengeance upon thee.

I'm not holding my breath on that last one.

---

*Not to be confused with the Grand Dragons of the KKK, though when you look at the voter suppression laws passed during the last session, it kind of makes you wonder...

Jeff Messer

Messerism #133

Let's face it, "Life, Liberty, and the Pursuit of Happiness" have pretty much been replaced by "Ignorance, Apathy, and abject Laziness."

Epilogue

I met the governor. That's right, I got to spend a few minutes with none other than Puppet Pat McCrory himself. On August 28, while the Moral Monday folks were marking the anniversary of the Martin Luther King, Jr. speech in Washington, DC, with a march to Raleigh, the governor was in Asheville.

Word came a few days prior that he would be stopping by the radio station for an on-air visit with Pete Kaliner on 570 AM. I knew that I had little chance of talking him into stopping by my studio (right next to Pete's) for a conversation with the progressive audience, but I also knew that this was a golden opportunity for some merry-making. I can see from my studio into Pete's through a big glass window, and I knew it would be a lot of fun to take selfies through the window, in a sort of reverse photo-bombing, while Pat hung out with Pete.

My producer, Seth Stewart, and I took some photos once the governor arrived, trying to be a little silly with it, and we chatted about it on air. To my surprise, at the commercial break, Program Director Brian Hall motioned me to come into Pete's studio to meet the governor. How could I pass this up?

I entered and introduced myself, shaking McCrory's hand, and identifying myself as "the other side of the conversation." To which McCrory queried: "Are you progressive or liberal? I don't understand the difference."

"I prefer to think of myself as pragmatic and common sense," I replied.

His aide pointed out that I was wearing a Tea Party T-shirt. Indeed, I was wearing a shirt with the "Join or Die" logo on the back.

"Original Tea Party," I said quickly. "1775."

I went to hand the governor my business card, which he mistook for another handshake move, which led to a moment of awkwardness.

I took note of McCrory's no-socks look, as he was decked out in deck shoes and khakis and a blue polo-type shirt. I commented on his casual look. I invited him to come on my show on 880, and said his visit didn't even have to be political. I told him I did a lot of culture and arts stuff and music and asked if he played any instruments.

"I used to play the drums a little," he said.

"Great," I replied. "I'll have you on, then take you down to the drum circle downtown."

Pete mentioned that I was writing a book.

To which McCrory said, looking at me: "Am I in it?"

"Oh, yeah," I replied. "Though you're not featured quite as much as your pal Tim."

"Tim? Moffitt?"

"Yeah. But I don't think you'll have to worry about him after November," I said.

McCrory played dumb. "Is his race not going well?

"He's down by eleven points in the polls."

Pete jumped in, quickly, "Those polls are way off."

There was some sparring about polling, and how McCrory had overcome negative polling.

I knew that I needed to get something good out of him, as far as possible quotes to use in this book, so I quickly circled back to it.

"My book is a political satire book about NC over the past few years," I said. "It's called *Red-state White-Guy Blues*."

"Isn't that racist?" asked McCrory, continuing to play (?) dumb.

There was a bit of laughter at this.

"What did I do?" McCrory asked, shifting a bit, "I went out there with a shovel." (He was referring to the Dan River spill).

"Were you digging up or covering up?" I asked quickly, getting in a jab.

McCrory either didn't hear me, or chose to ignore the comment, and asked if I thought people wanted to see him out there with coal soot all over his hands.

"I'm sure that could be Photoshopped in," I said.

From my studio, Seth signal me that we were coming back on air. I needed to wind things up fast.

"Anytime you want to come over to 880 and see how the other half lives, let me know. I'd love to have you," I offered. "Plus, now that Pete's sporting the skinhead look [he shaved it for charity last December], hanging with him might give you an even worse reputation." A slight chuckle came, and I turned to the bald aide near the door, and said to him, "No offense."

With that, I went back to my show on 880, feeling good about getting in a few jabs on the governor, who clearly didn't want to open up to any serious conversation.

I would love to have been able to ask him a few serious questions, like about his views on raising the minimum wage in light of his comments about $31,000 not being enough to live on for teachers starting out; or perhaps about whether or not the fracking push in NC was a smokescreen for something more dubious coming down the pipeline (figuratively and literally); or perhaps about the people in NC who were dead or would die because of his lack of willingness to expand Medicaid. But, alas, it was not meant to be.

However, he will be getting a copy of this book from me for Christmas this year. That you can count on.

Jeff Messer

About the Author

Jeff Douglas Messer started writing at a young age with his fifth-grade Spring Play. A more professional success came a decade later when Haywood Arts Regional Theatre in his hometown of Waynesville, NC produced his play about Irving Berlin, the first script ever approved about the famed composer.

Many of his plays found their way to becoming finalists in play competitions, and in 2000 *Robin Hood, The Legend of Sherwood* (co-authored with Robert Akers) earned commercial and critical success; the play spawned a series of scripts based on the legend, and plans are in motion to create a series of radio dramas based on them.

Jeff opened his own theater company in Asheville, NC in 2002. Other collaborations included a 2003 adaptation (co-written with Andrew Gall) of Bram Stoker's *Dracula*. In 2004, he worked with the Thomas Wolfe Association to bring to life Wolfe's first play, *Welcome To Our City*, editing the hefty script and adapting it for a smaller cast.

In 2008, Jeff's anti-Iraq War play, *This War Is Live*, premiered at the Footlight in Charleston, SC, followed in 2009 by his bio-play *Esley: The Life and Music of Lesley Riddle* for Parkway Playhouse, in Burnsville, NC. 2013 brought his original Sherlock Holmes adventure, *Sherlock Holmes Returns, or the Curse of the Bloody Heart*, to Parkway's stage.

A life-long fan of comic books, Jeff is also working on an adaptation of Mike Grell's "Jon Sable" character for stage, and has high hopes of breaking into the comics industry as a writer himself, bringing the Robin Hood and Sherlock Holmes scripts over to that medium, as well as prose versions of the material.

Jeff is married and lives with his wife, Kelli, her two kids, and his son, in Asheville, NC.

Pisgah Press

Also available from Pisgah Press

Mombie, the Zombie Mom — Barry A. Burgess
$16.95 — illustrated by Jake LaGory

Letting Go: Collected Poems 1983-2003 — Donna Lisle Burton
$14.95

MacTiernan's Bottle — Michael Hopping
$14.95

rhythms on a flaming drum — Michael Hopping
$16.95

I Like It Here! Adventures in the Wild & Wonderful World of Theatre — C. Robert Jones
$30.00

Lanky Tales, Vol. I: The Bird Man & Other Stories — C. Robert Jones
$9.00 — illustrated by Jennie Jones Branham

Fragments — Martin A. Keeley
$16.00

Oscar & the Royal Avenue Cats — Martin A. Keeley
$15.00

A Green One for Woody — Patrick O'Sullivan
$15.95

Reed's Homophones: a comprehensive book of sound-alike words — A. D. Reed
$10.00

Swords in their Hands: George Washington and the Newburgh Conspiracy — Dave Richards
$24.95

Trang Sen: A Novel of Viet Nam — Sarah-Ann Smith
$19.50

To order:

Pisgah Press, LLC
PO Box 1427, Candler, NC 28715
www.pisgahpress.com